Communicating with Data
ESSENTIALS EDITION

Kimberly Seefeld, EdD

Table of contents

Communicating with Data

ESSENTIALS EDITION

By Kimberly Seefeld, EdD

Published under **DataJoyAI** imprint

Edition: First Edition
ISBN: 978-1-969233-24-1

Chapter 1

Foundations of Data Communication

1.1 Introduction

Picture this: A data analyst discovers that customer satisfaction scores have dropped by 15% over the past quarter, but when they present this critical finding in a dense spreadsheet filled with numbers, the executive team's eyes glaze over, and no action is taken. Three months later, the company loses its largest client due to unaddressed service issues. This scenario plays out in organizations worldwide every day, highlighting a fundamental truth: data without effective communication is just expensive noise.

In our hyperconnected world, where businesses generate over 2.5 quintillion bytes of data daily, the ability to transform raw information into compelling, actionable insights has become the defining skill that separates successful organizations from those that struggle to compete . According to McKinsey research, over 60% of businesses struggle to transform their vast data streams into actionable insights, leaving millions of dollars in opportunity on the table . The problem isn't a lack of data—it's the failure to communicate that data effectively.

Data communication represents the critical bridge between raw information and informed decision-making. It encompasses not just the technical aspects of how data moves between systems, but more importantly, how we transform complex datasets into clear, compelling narratives that drive action. Whether you're presenting quarterly sales figures to the board, explaining customer behavior patterns to the marketing team, or sharing operational insights with frontline managers, your ability to communicate data effectively determines whether your analysis creates value or gets ignored.

The stakes have never been higher. In 2025, organizations that master data communication enjoy significant competitive advantages: they make decisions 5x faster than their competitors, achieve 23% higher profitability, and demonstrate 19% better accuracy in forecasting . Conversely, organizations that struggle with data communication face delayed decisions, missed opportunities, and the constant frustration of having valuable insights that never translate into action.

This transformation from data to insight to action doesn't happen by accident—it requires mastering the foundational principles of effective data communication. These principles encompass understanding your audience and their needs, selecting appropriate formats and visualizations, crafting compelling narratives around your data, and ensuring that your message is not only heard but understood and acted upon.

As future data analytics professionals, you will be the translators who help organizations make sense of their data landscape. Your technical skills in analysis and modeling are essential, but your ability to communicate findings effectively will determine your impact and career success. The most brilliant analysis in the world creates no value if it cannot be understood and acted upon by decision-makers.

1.2 The Critical Importance of Data Communication

In the modern business landscape, data communication serves as the nervous system of organizational intelligence, connecting insights generated by analysis to the decisions that drive business outcomes. Understanding why effective data communication matters—and what happens when it fails—provides the foundation for developing expertise in this critical skill.

1.2.1 The Business Case for Effective Data Communication

The economic impact of effective data communication extends far beyond individual presentations or reports. Organizations that excel at data communication demonstrate measurably superior performance across multiple dimensions. Research from leading consulting firms reveals that data-driven organizations are 23 times more likely to acquire customers, 6 times more likely to retain customers, and 19 times more likely to be profitable . However, these benefits only materialize when data insights are effectively communicated and acted upon.

Consider the transformation at Netflix, where data communication excellence enabled the company to shift from DVD rentals to streaming dominance. Netflix doesn't just collect viewing data—they communicate insights about viewer preferences so effectively that content creators, marketing teams, and executives can make coordinated decisions that result in hit shows and satisfied customers. Their data communication approach transforms complex viewing patterns into clear strategic directions that every stakeholder can understand and act upon.

The speed of decision-making represents another critical advantage of effective data communication. In today's fast-paced business environment, the ability to quickly communicate insights can mean the difference between capturing market opportunities and watching competitors seize them. Organizations with strong data communication capabilities make decisions 5 times faster than their peers, primarily because stakeholders can quickly understand and act on presented information rather than spending time deciphering unclear or poorly presented data .

1.2.2 The Hidden Costs of Poor Data Communication

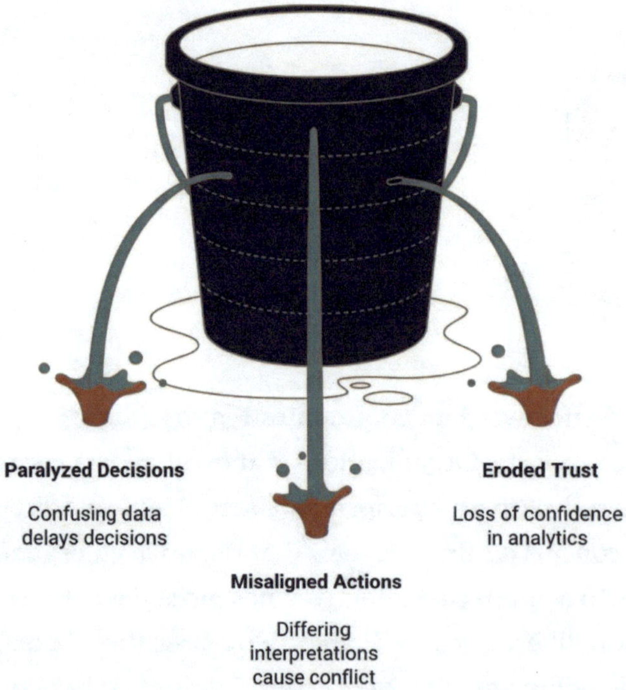

The consequences of ineffective data communication extend far beyond missed opportunities—they create cascading problems that can undermine entire organizational strategies. When data insights are poorly communicated, several costly problems emerge that organizations often fail to recognize or address systematically.

Decision paralysis occurs when stakeholders receive data that is technically accurate but practically incomprehensible. Faced with unclear or overwhelming information, decision-makers often delay choices, request additional analysis, or make decisions based on intuition rather than data. This paralysis is particularly costly in dynamic markets where timing is crucial for competitive advantage.

Misaligned actions represent another significant cost of poor data communication. When different stakeholders interpret the same data differently due to unclear communication, they may take contradictory actions that work against organizational goals. For example, if sales data is communicated in a way that suggests different priorities to the sales team versus the marketing team, their efforts may conflict rather than reinforce each other.

The erosion of trust in data and analytics represents perhaps the most insidious cost of poor data communication. When stakeholders repeatedly receive data communications that are confusing, contradictory, or irrelevant to their needs, they begin to discount the value of data-driven insights altogether. This erosion of trust can take years to rebuild and may cause organizations to revert to intuition-based decision-making even when superior data insights are available.

1.2.3 Data Communication as Competitive Advantage

Organizations that master data communication create sustainable competitive advantages that are difficult for competitors to replicate. These advantages manifest in multiple ways that compound over time to create significant market differentiation.

Enhanced organizational learning occurs when data insights are communicated effectively throughout the organization. When insights from one department or project are clearly communicated and understood by others, the entire organization becomes smarter and more capable. This collective learning accelerates innovation and helps organizations avoid repeating mistakes or missing opportunities to apply successful strategies in new contexts.

Improved stakeholder confidence emerges when data communications consistently provide clear, actionable insights that lead to positive outcomes. Stakeholders—whether internal teams, executives, investors, or customers—develop confidence in the organization's analytical capabilities and decision-making processes. This confidence translates into increased support for data-driven initiatives and greater willingness to act on analytical recommendations.

Accelerated innovation results from effective data communication that helps teams quickly identify patterns, opportunities, and problems. When insights are communicated clearly and promptly, teams can iterate faster, test new approaches more efficiently, and scale successful innovations more rapidly than competitors who struggle with data communication.

1.2.4 The Evolution of Data Communication Expectations

The expectations for data communication have evolved dramatically as organizations become more data-literate and as analytical tools become more sophisticated. Understanding these evolving expectations is crucial for developing relevant data communication skills.

Modern stakeholders expect data communications to be not just accurate but also timely, relevant, and actionable. The days when analysts could simply present data and leave interpretation to others are largely over. Today's stakeholders expect data communications to provide clear insights, recommend specific actions, and explain the reasoning behind recommendations.

The democratization of analytical tools has also raised expectations for data communication quality. As more stakeholders gain access to self-service analytics platforms, they develop higher standards for what constitutes effective data communication. They expect professional-quality visualizations, clear narratives, and insights that go beyond what they could discover themselves using basic analytical tools.

Real-time expectations have become increasingly common as organizations implement systems that can provide up-to-the-minute data. Stakeholders now expect data communications to reflect current conditions rather than historical snapshots, and they expect to receive updates as conditions change rather than waiting for scheduled reports.

1.3 Core Principles of Effective Data Communication

Mastering data communication requires understanding and applying fundamental principles that guide all successful communication efforts. These principles provide the framework for transforming raw data into compelling, actionable insights that drive organizational success.

1.3.1 Principle 1: Know Your Audience Deeply

Effective data communication begins with profound understanding of your audience—not just their roles and responsibilities, but their goals, constraints, decision-making processes, and information preferences. This understanding shapes every aspect of how you present data, from the level of detail you include to the format you choose to the language you use.

Audience analysis extends beyond basic demographics to encompass cognitive preferences, time constraints, and decision-making authority. Executives typically prefer high-level insights with clear implications for strategic decisions, while operational managers need detailed information that helps them optimize day-to-day processes. Technical teams may appreciate methodological details and statistical rigor, while sales teams focus on actionable insights that help them close deals.

Understanding your audience's existing knowledge and biases is equally important. If your audience already believes strongly in a particular course of action, your data communication must acknowledge this perspective while presenting evidence that either supports or challenges their assumptions. Ignoring existing beliefs or presenting contradictory evidence without proper context often leads to rejection of even the most compelling data insights.

The decision-making context significantly influences how you should communicate data. Audiences making urgent decisions need concise, clear recommendations with minimal supporting detail, while audiences making strategic decisions with long-term implications may require comprehensive analysis with multiple scenarios and detailed supporting evidence. Matching your communication approach to the decision-making context ensures that your insights are both relevant and actionable .

1.3.2 Principle 2: Lead with Clarity and Simplicity

Clarity represents the foundation of all effective data communication. No matter how sophisticated your analysis or how compelling your insights, unclear communication renders your work ineffective. Clarity in data communication means that your audience can quickly understand your key messages without confusion or misinterpretation.

Simplicity does not mean oversimplification—it means presenting complex information in the most accessible way possible without losing essential meaning. This requires careful consideration of what information is truly necessary for your audience to understand and act on your insights. Every element in your communication should serve a clear purpose in advancing your message.

The principle of progressive disclosure helps maintain clarity while providing necessary detail. Start with your key insights and recommendations, then provide supporting evidence and methodology for audiences who need deeper understanding. This approach ensures that all audience members can quickly grasp your main points while allowing those who need additional detail to access it without overwhelming others.

Visual hierarchy plays a crucial role in achieving clarity. Use formatting, color, and layout to guide your audience's attention to the most important information first. Clear headings, consistent formatting, and strategic use of white space help audiences navigate your communication efficiently and focus on key insights .

1.3.3 Principle 3: Tell a Compelling Data Story

Data storytelling transforms static information into engaging narratives that connect with audiences emotionally and intellectually. Effective data stories follow narrative structures that help audiences understand not just what the data shows, but why it matters and what they should do about it.

Every compelling data story includes three essential elements: context that explains why the analysis matters, conflict that highlights problems or opportunities revealed by the data, and resolution that provides clear recommendations for action. This narrative structure helps audiences follow your reasoning and understand the implications of your findings.

The context element establishes the business situation or question that motivated your analysis. Without proper context, even the most interesting data insights may seem irrelevant or unimportant to your audience. Context should connect your analysis to broader organizational goals, market conditions, or strategic initiatives that your audience cares about.

Conflict in data stories doesn't mean controversy—it means tension between current conditions and desired outcomes, or between different possible interpretations of the data. This tension creates engagement and helps audiences understand why your analysis matters. For example, discovering that customer satisfaction is declining while sales are increasing creates productive tension that demands explanation and action.

Resolution provides the payoff for your data story by offering clear, actionable recommendations based on your analysis. Strong resolutions don't just summarize findings—they provide specific guidance about what actions to take, what outcomes to expect, and how to measure success .

1.3.4 Principle 4: Choose Appropriate Visual Elements

Visual elements in data communication serve specific purposes and should be selected based on the type of data you're presenting and the insights you want to emphasize. Understanding when and how to use different visual elements is crucial for effective data communication.

Chart selection should be driven by the nature of your data and the comparisons you want to highlight. Bar charts excel at comparing quantities across categories, line charts effectively show trends over time, scatter plots reveal relationships between variables, and pie charts can show proportions of a whole (though they should be used sparingly and only with a limited number of categories).

Color usage should be strategic and consistent throughout your communication. Use color to highlight important information, group related elements, or show progression, but avoid using too many colors that can overwhelm or confuse your audience. Ensure that your color choices are accessible to colorblind audience members and that they reproduce well in different formats.

Typography and layout contribute significantly to the effectiveness of your data communication. Consistent fonts, appropriate sizing, and clear hierarchy help audiences navigate your content efficiently. Adequate white space prevents visual clutter and helps important elements stand out.

The principle of data-ink ratio, introduced by Edward Tufte, suggests maximizing the proportion of ink used to display actual data while minimizing decorative or non-essential elements. This principle helps create clean, focused visualizations that emphasize insights rather than design elements .

1.3.5 Principle 5: Ensure Accuracy and Integrity

Accuracy in data communication extends beyond ensuring that numbers are correct—it encompasses presenting data in ways that accurately represent the underlying reality and don't mislead audiences through poor design choices or selective presentation.

Statistical integrity requires presenting data with appropriate context, including sample sizes, confidence intervals, and limitations of the analysis. Audiences need to understand the reliability and scope of your findings to make appropriate decisions based on your insights.

Visual integrity means avoiding design choices that distort the perception of your data. This includes using appropriate scales, avoiding truncated axes that exaggerate differences, and ensuring that visual elements are proportional to the data they represent.

Transparency about methodology, assumptions, and limitations builds trust with your audience and helps them understand the appropriate applications of your insights. Being upfront about what your analysis can and cannot tell them demonstrates professional integrity and helps prevent misuse of your findings.

1.4 Common Data Communication Formats

The format you choose for communicating data significantly impacts how effectively your message reaches and influences your audience. Understanding the strengths, limitations, and appropriate applications of different communication formats enables you to select the most effective approach for each situation.

1.4.1 Visual Communication Formats

Visual formats represent the most powerful and widely used approaches for data communication, leveraging the human brain's exceptional ability to process visual information quickly and identify patterns. However, the effectiveness of visual communication depends heavily on choosing the right type of visualization for your data and message.

Static Visualizations form the foundation of most data communication efforts. Charts, graphs, and infographics can convey complex information quickly and memorably when designed effectively. Bar charts excel at comparing quantities across categories, making them ideal for showing sales performance across regions or customer satisfaction scores across departments. Line charts effectively communicate trends over time, helping audiences understand whether key metrics are improving, declining, or remaining stable.

Scatter plots reveal relationships between variables that might not be apparent in other formats, making them valuable for exploratory analysis and hypothesis testing. Heat maps can show patterns across multiple dimensions simultaneously, such as website traffic patterns by day of week and time of day. The key to effective static visualizations is matching the chart type to both your data structure and the insights you want to emphasize.

Interactive Visualizations enable audiences to explore data dynamically, filtering, drilling down, and examining different perspectives based on their interests and needs. Dashboards represent the most common form of interactive data communication, providing real-time or near-real-time views of key performance indicators that stakeholders can monitor and explore.

Interactive elements should enhance understanding rather than simply providing novelty. Effective interactive visualizations include filtering capabilities that help audiences focus on relevant subsets of data, drill-down functionality that allows exploration of summary data in greater detail, and comparison tools that enable side-by-side analysis of different time periods, regions, or segments.

The design of interactive visualizations requires careful consideration of user experience principles. Navigation should be intuitive, loading times should be minimal, and the interface should guide users toward the most important insights while allowing flexibility for exploration .

1.4.2 Textual Communication Formats

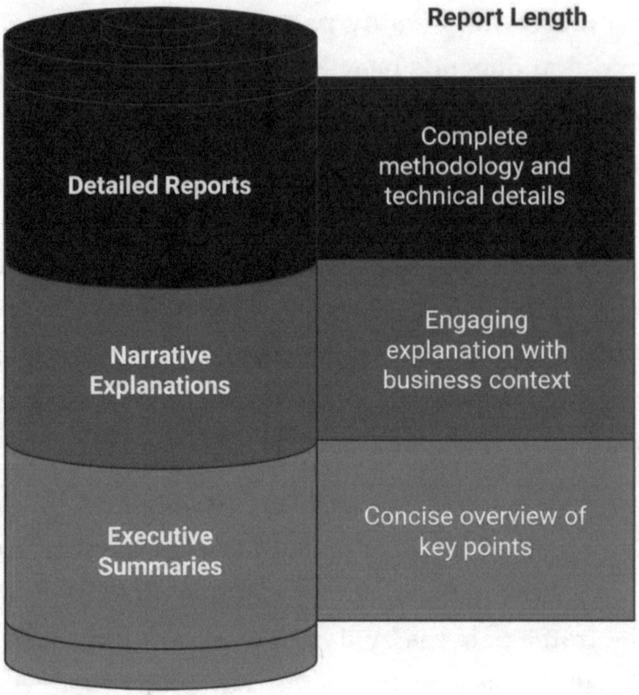

While visual formats often receive the most attention in data communication, textual formats remain essential for providing context, explaining methodology, and delivering detailed recommendations that require nuanced explanation.

Executive Summaries distill complex analyses into concise overviews that busy stakeholders can quickly consume. Effective executive summaries lead with key findings and recommendations, provide essential context, and include enough supporting detail to build confidence without overwhelming the reader. The typical executive summary should be readable in 2-3 minutes while providing sufficient information for decision-making.

The structure of executive summaries should follow a logical flow: situation or context, key findings, implications, and recommended actions. Each section should be concise but complete, avoiding jargon or technical terms that might confuse non-technical audiences. Bullet points and numbered lists can help organize information and make it easier to scan quickly.

Detailed Reports serve audiences who need comprehensive information to understand methodology, validate findings, or implement recommendations. These reports should be well-organized with clear sections, informative headings, and logical flow from problem definition through analysis to conclusions and recommendations.

Effective detailed reports balance comprehensiveness with readability. They include sufficient methodological detail for replication and validation while maintaining focus on insights and implications. Appendices can house technical details that support the analysis without interrupting the main narrative flow.

Narrative Explanations help audiences understand the story behind the data, connecting analytical findings to business context and strategic implications. These explanations should be engaging and accessible while maintaining analytical rigor. They often work best when combined with visual elements that support and illustrate key points.

1.4.3 Hybrid Communication Formats

The most effective data communications often combine multiple formats, leveraging the strengths of each while offsetting individual limitations. Hybrid approaches provide both immediate impact and comprehensive detail, accommodating different audience preferences and information needs.

Presentation formats pair visual elements with narrative explanation, allowing presenters to guide audiences through complex information and encourage questions and discussion. Effective presentations follow storytelling principles, moving from context through analysis to conclusions and recommendations. Slides should support the presenter with minimal text, focusing on key data points, and using animation only to enhance understanding.

Dashboard reports merge real-time interactive visualizations with written commentary. They let users explore trends while highlighting key insights and actionable recommendations. This format balances situational awareness with analytical depth.

Infographic reports combine visual appeal with substantive analysis, making research findings accessible and engaging for broad audiences. Clear visuals paired with concise explanations allow complex data to be understood without losing rigor or insight.

1.4.4 Format Selection Criteria

Choosing the right format for data communication requires considering audience, data, objectives, and organizational context. Audience characteristics are key: technical audiences may value detailed methodology, while business audiences prefer clear insights and actionable recommendations. Time-constrained audiences need concise formats, whereas complex decision-making may require comprehensive detail.

Data characteristics also guide format choice. Simple comparisons suit basic charts, while multidimensional data may need interactive visualizations or detailed reports. Time-series data fits line charts; categorical data works well in bar charts or tables.

Communication objectives drive decisions. To inform, use detailed reports or dashboards; to persuade, employ storytelling with compelling visuals; to enable ongoing monitoring, interactive dashboards are ideal. Organizational context—preferences, tools, and technical constraints—also shapes which formats will be effective and actionable..

1.5 Building Effective Data Communication Strategies

Effective data communication requires more than creating charts or writing reports. It involves planning, execution, and evaluation to ensure your insights are understood, trusted, and acted upon.

1.5.1 Strategic Planning

Planning starts with understanding your stakeholders. Different groups have different needs: executives often want concise, high-level takeaways; managers may need detailed instructions for implementation; technical teams care about methodology; and other teams may focus on practical implications. Mapping out your stakeholders ensures you deliver the right information to the right people.

Next, define clear objectives. Are you aiming to inform, persuade, or enable ongoing monitoring? Objectives should be specific and measurable. For example, "help the marketing team reallocate 20% of the budget to digital channels this quarter" is clearer than simply "communicate findings."

Assess your resources before you begin. Time, tools, and expertise influence which formats and approaches are realistic. Limited resources might require focusing on key insights, while more abundant resources allow multi-format communications that reach multiple audiences.

1.5.2 Execution Best Practices

Start with your main insights, then identify supporting evidence and context. Drafts should focus on getting ideas down; subsequent revisions refine clarity, accuracy, and visual appeal. Testing your communication with a small group can catch confusing points early.

Quality assurance is critical. Check data accuracy, visual consistency, and message clarity. Peer review is invaluable—fresh eyes often spot unclear explanations or gaps in logic.

Delivery matters as much as content. Choose formats and channels that match audience needs, whether presentations, reports, dashboards, or infographics. Timing and follow-up are also important. Make sure stakeholders understand the implications, could ask questions, and can act on recommendations.

1.5.3 Measuring Communication Effectiveness

Assess both immediate and long-term outcomes. Immediate feedback, such as questions or requests for clarification, shows how well your message is understood. Engagement metrics, like dashboard use or report access, give quantitative insight.

he most important measure is impact: do stakeholders act on your recommendations? Are decisions made faster or more effectively? Over time, effective communication builds organizational learning, improves decision-making quality, and strengthens confidence in analytical work. Clear, actionable communication creates a positive cycle: the better your messages, the more your organization values and uses data.

1.6 Industry Standards and Best Practices

Professional data communication benefits from established standards and frameworks that ensure consistency, quality, and effectiveness across different contexts and organizations. Understanding and applying these standards helps create communications that meet professional expectations while maximizing impact.

1.6.1 International Business Communication Standards (IBCS)

The International Business Communication Standards (IBCS) provide comprehensive guidelines for creating clear, consistent, and effective business communications, particularly for reports and presentations that include quantitative information. Developed by Professor Rolf Hichert and refined by the IBCS Association, these standards address common problems in business communication through systematic rules and principles .

The SUCCESS Formula forms the core of IBCS methodology, providing a systematic approach to communication design. SUCCESS stands for Say, Unify, Condense, Check, Express, Simplify, and Structure—seven principles that guide the creation of effective business communications.

Say (Simplify) focuses on defining clear messages before beginning communication design. This principle emphasizes the importance of knowing what you want to communicate and ensuring that every element of your communication supports that message. Without clear message definition, communications often become unfocused and ineffective.

Unify ensures consistency in symbols, colors, and terminology across all communications. This consistency helps audiences quickly understand and compare information across different reports and presentations. Unified approaches reduce cognitive load and prevent misinterpretation due to inconsistent design choices.

Condense emphasizes the importance of presenting information concisely without losing essential meaning. This principle helps communicators focus on what matters most while avoiding information overload that can overwhelm audiences and obscure key insights.

Check involves systematic review to ensure that communications meet quality standards and effectively convey intended messages. This includes both technical accuracy and communication effectiveness review.

Express focuses on using clear and meaningful visualizations that effectively convey messages. This principle guides the selection of appropriate chart types, visual elements, and design approaches that enhance rather than hinder understanding.

Simplify reduces complex information to essential elements while maintaining accuracy and completeness. This principle helps create communications that are accessible to broad audiences without oversimplifying important nuances.

Structure organizes information logically and clearly to facilitate easy navigation and understanding. Well-structured communications guide audiences through complex information in ways that build understanding progressively.

1.6.2 Data Visualization Best Practices

Professional data visualization follows established principles that ensure clarity, accuracy, and effectiveness across different contexts and audiences. These principles have been developed through research in cognitive psychology, design theory, and practical experience across many industries.

Visual Hierarchy guides audience attention to the most important information first through strategic use of size, color, position, and contrast. Effective visual hierarchy ensures that key insights are immediately apparent while supporting details are available for audiences who need them.

Primary information should be the most visually prominent, using larger fonts, brighter colors, or central positioning to draw attention. Secondary information should be clearly visible but less prominent, while tertiary details should be available but not distracting from main messages.

Color Strategy uses color purposefully to enhance understanding rather than simply for aesthetic appeal. Effective color strategies assign specific meanings to colors and use them consistently throughout communications. For example, green might always represent positive performance while red indicates problems or concerns.

Color accessibility ensures that communications are effective for audiences with color vision deficiencies. This typically involves using color combinations that provide sufficient contrast and avoiding reliance on color alone to convey important information. Patterns, shapes, or labels can supplement color coding to ensure accessibility.

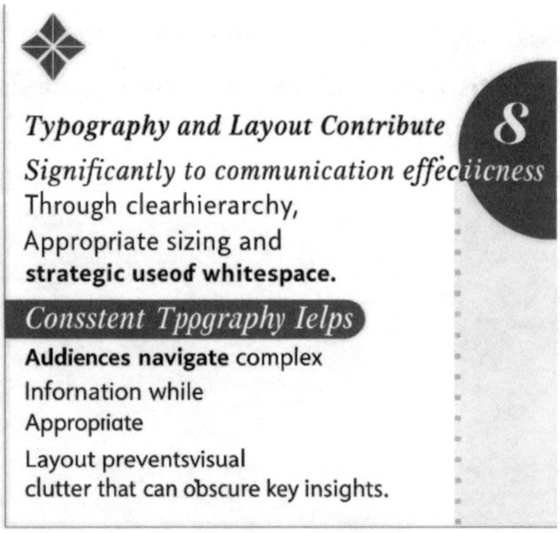

Typography and Layout contribute significantly to communication effectiveness through clear hierarchy, appropriate sizing, and strategic use of white space. Consistent typography helps audiences navigate complex information while appropriate layout prevents visual clutter that can obscure key insights.

Font selection should prioritize readability over novelty, with consistent use of font families and sizes throughout communications. Adequate white space prevents visual crowding and helps important elements stand out clearly .

1.6.3 Quality Assurance Frameworks

Systematic quality assurance ensures that data communications meet professional standards for accuracy, clarity, and effectiveness. Quality frameworks provide structured approaches to reviewing and improving communications before delivery to stakeholders.

Technical Accuracy Review verifies that all data, calculations, and analytical methods are correct and appropriate. This includes checking data sources, validating calculations, and ensuring that analytical approaches are suitable for the questions being addressed.

Data lineage documentation helps ensure that data sources are reliable and that any transformations or calculations are properly applied. Understanding where data comes from and how it has been processed is essential for maintaining accuracy and building stakeholder confidence.

Communication Effectiveness Review evaluates whether communications successfully convey intended messages to target audiences. This review considers clarity, organization, visual design, and alignment with audience needs and preferences.

Message testing with representative audience members can identify areas of confusion or misinterpretation before final delivery. This testing helps ensure that communications are not only technically accurate but also practically effective.

Compliance and Ethics Review ensures that communications meet organizational standards and ethical guidelines for data use and presentation. This includes verifying that data privacy requirements are met, that presentations are fair and unbiased, and that any limitations or uncertainties are appropriately disclosed.

Professional ethics in data communication require transparency about methodology, honest presentation of findings, and acknowledgment of limitations or uncertainties. Building trust through ethical communication practices creates long-term value that extends beyond individual projects .

1.7 Conclusion

You've now built the essential foundation for effective data communication, a skill that transforms analytical work into real organizational impact. Technical expertise alone is not enough—insights only create value when they are clearly understood and actionable by decision-makers.

The principles you've learned—understanding your audience, leading with clarity, telling compelling stories, selecting appropriate visuals, and maintaining accuracy—form a framework that will serve you throughout your career. Your ability to choose and combine formats strategically, plan communications aligned with stakeholder needs and uphold professional and ethical standards will distinguish you as a trusted and effective data professional.

As data grows in volume and complexity, organizations that communicate insights well will maintain a competitive edge. Integrating communication skills with technical analysis gives you a rare and valuable advantage in the job market. Collaboration, ethical responsibility, and adaptability will remain central as you apply these skills across diverse teams and evolving technologies.

The foundation you've built here is just the beginning. Each report, presentation, and analysis is an opportunity to refine your craft, transform data into understanding, and make decisions that positively impact organizations and people. Mastering data communication ensures that your work doesn't just produce numbers—it drives meaningful action.

Chapter 2

Design Elements and Their Impact

2.1 Introduction

Picture this scenario: Two data analysts walk into the same boardroom to present identical findings to the same executive team. The first analyst displays a cluttered chart filled with tiny labels, clashing neon colors, and no clear focal point. The executives squint at the screen, struggle to follow the logic, and ultimately dismiss the insights as too confusing to act upon. The second analyst presents the exact same data using clear visual hierarchy, an accessible color palette, and thoughtful typography. The executives immediately grasp the key insights, ask strategic questions, and approve the recommended actions within minutes.

The difference between these two outcomes wasn't the quality of the analysis, the importance of the insights, or even the presentation skills of the analysts. The difference was design. This scenario illustrates a fundamental truth about data communication that many professionals learn too late in their careers: content may be king, but design is the crown that makes it visible, accessible, and actionable.

In our increasingly visual world, where decision-makers process information at unprecedented speeds, the design elements you choose can determine whether your insights create meaningful impact or get lost in the noise. Poor design doesn't just make data harder to understand—it can actively mislead audiences, exclude users with disabilities, and undermine the credibility of even the most rigorous analysis.

2.2 Why Design Matters More Than You Think

2.2.1 Science Behind Visual Impact

Research reveals some startling facts about how humans process visual information. Well-designed data visualizations are processed sixty thousand times faster than text, while poorly designed ones can lead to misinterpretation rates as high as thirty percent. Perhaps most remarkably, first impressions of visual designs form in just fifty milliseconds—faster than the blink of an eye. These findings underscore a crucial reality: in our visually driven world, design competency has become as important as analytical skills for data professionals.

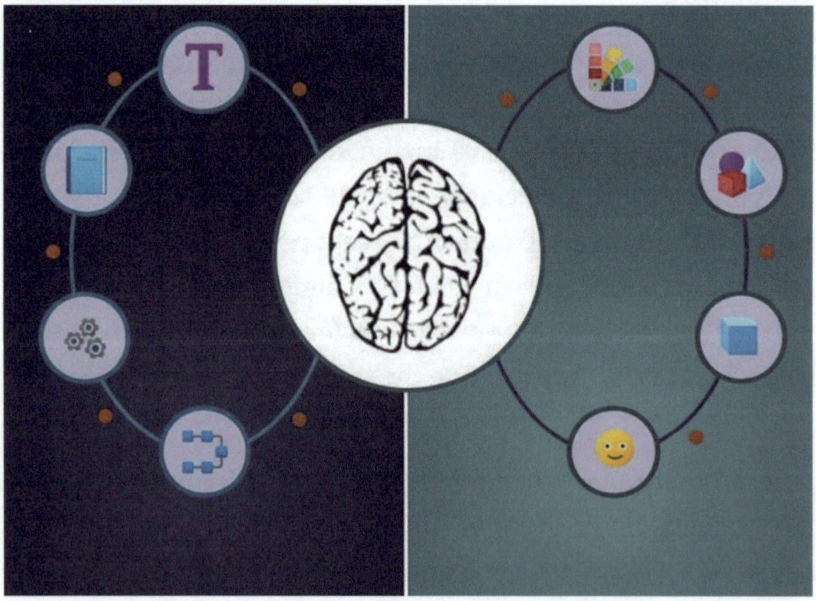

The implications for your career are profound. While technical skills, analytical abilities, and statistical knowledge may get you hired, it's your communication skills, design competency, and ability to influence decisions that will determine your long-term impact and advancement. The most sophisticated statistical models and comprehensive datasets create no value if they cannot be communicated effectively through thoughtful, accessible design.

Consider the reality that ninety percent of all information transmitted to the human brain is visual. This biological fact means that the form of presented information is often more important than the information itself. Your audience's brain will make critical decisions about the importance and credibility of your work before they even consciously begin to analyze your content.

2.2.2 The Three Pillars of Design Success

Effective data visualization design rests on three fundamental pillars that work together to create compelling, accessible communications. Visual design basics provide the foundation, establishing principles of hierarchy, balance, and emphasis that guide viewers through complex information. Labels and formatting serve as the navigation system, helping audiences understand what they're seeing and how to interpret it correctly. Accessibility considerations ensure that your communications reach and serve all users, regardless of their abilities or the technologies they use to access information.

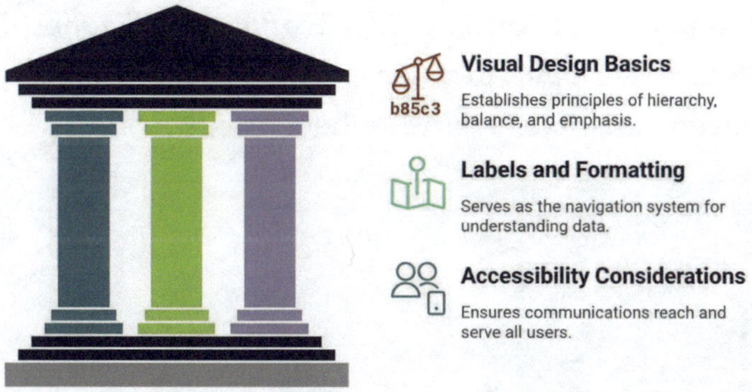

These three pillars are interconnected and mutually reinforcing. Strong visual design principles become meaningless if your labels are confusing or your formatting is inconsistent. Clear labels and formatting lose their effectiveness if your design violates accessibility standards that prevent some users from accessing your content. Accessibility considerations must be built into your visual design choices from the beginning, not added as an afterthought.

Understanding this interconnected relationship will transform how you approach data visualization projects. Instead of treating design as decoration applied after analysis is complete, you'll begin to see design as an integral part of the analytical process itself—a way of thinking through your data that reveals insights and communicates them simultaneously.

2.3 Visual Design Basics: Your Foundation

2.3.1 How Your Brain Sees Data

Understanding how humans process visual information provides the scientific foundation for all effective design decisions. The human visual system has evolved over millions of years to quickly identify patterns, detect changes, and prioritize information based on visual cues. This biological inheritance creates predictable responses to visual stimuli that skilled designers can leverage to guide attention and enhance comprehension.

Pre-attentive processing occurs in the first two hundred to five hundred milliseconds of viewing, before conscious attention is directed to specific elements. During this crucial phase, your brain automatically processes basic visual attributes like color, motion, size, and position. Effective data visualization design leverages these pre-attentive attributes to guide attention to the most important information before viewers consciously decide where to look.

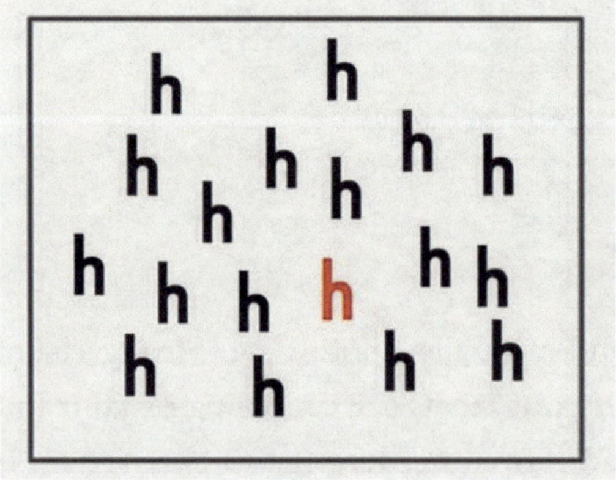

This process explains why certain design choices feel immediately intuitive while others require conscious effort to understand. When you make an element larger, use a bright color, or position something in the upper left corner of a Western-oriented design, you're working with your audience's pre-attentive processing system rather than against it. Conversely, when you use random colors, inconsistent sizing, or chaotic positioning, you're forcing viewers to work harder to understand your message.

Color serves as one of the most powerful pre-attentive attributes, with the human eye capable of distinguishing millions of different hues. However, this capability comes with important limitations and considerations that affect design decisions. Approximately eight percent of men and half a percent of women have some form of color vision deficiency, making color-only encoding problematic for accessibility. Additionally, cultural associations with colors can influence interpretation, with red often signifying danger or negative values in Western cultures while representing good fortune in many Asian cultures.

2.3.2 The Gestalt Principles in Action

The Gestalt principles describe how humans naturally group and organize visual elements, providing a psychological foundation for effective design choices. These principles, developed by early twentieth-century psychologists, explain why certain visual arrangements feel natural and comprehensible while others appear chaotic or confusing.

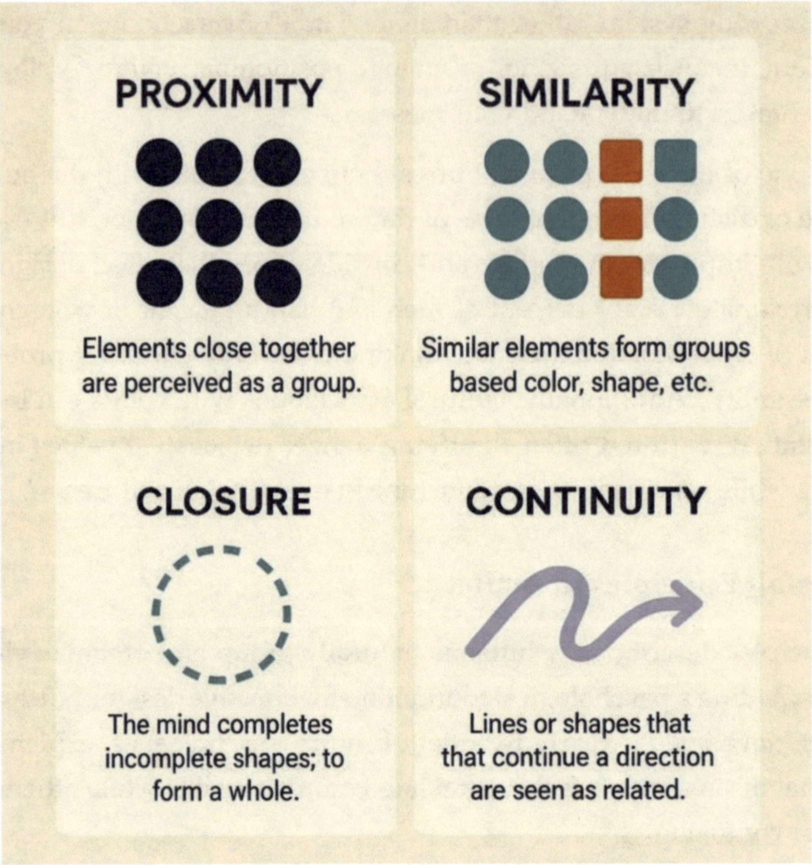

The principle of proximity suggests that elements placed close together are perceived as related, making it highly effective for grouping related data points or categories in visualizations. When you position related chart elements near each other and separate different categories with white space, you're leveraging this natural tendency to help viewers understand relationships without conscious effort.

Similarity indicates that elements sharing visual characteristics such as color, shape, or size are perceived as belonging to the same group. This principle proves invaluable for creating visual categories in complex datasets. When you use the same color for all data points representing the same category, or the same shape for all elements serving the same function, you're helping viewers automatically organize information into meaningful groups.

The principle of closure explains why humans tend to complete incomplete shapes or patterns, which can be leveraged in data visualization to reduce visual clutter while maintaining comprehension. You can use this principle to create cleaner designs by removing unnecessary chart borders or grid lines, trusting that viewers will mentally complete the implied structure.

Continuity suggests that elements arranged in smooth, continuous lines or curves are perceived as related, making it particularly effective for showing trends or relationships over time. This principle explains why line charts feel so natural for temporal data and why smooth curves often communicate trends more effectively than jagged, angular lines.

2.4 Visual Hierarchy: Guiding the Eye

2.4.1 The Power of Size and Scale

Visual hierarchy represents the most critical design principle for data communication, determining the order in which viewers process information and the relative importance they assign to different elements. Effective hierarchy ensures that the most important insights are noticed first and that supporting information is available without overwhelming the primary message.

Size and scale provide the most direct method for establishing hierarchy, with larger elements naturally drawing more attention than smaller ones. In data visualization, this principle can be applied through varying chart sizes, font sizes, or the thickness of lines and borders. However, size relationships must be proportional to the data they represent to maintain accuracy and avoid misleading viewers.

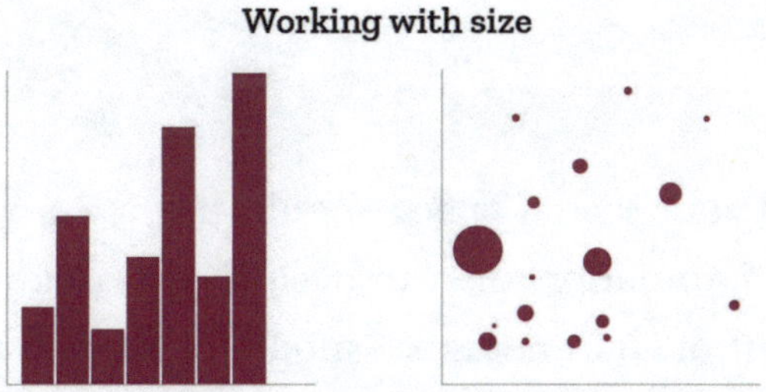

Consider how Netflix structures their analytics dashboards. The main metric—subscriber growth—appears in large, bold typography that immediately draws attention. Supporting metrics like engagement rates and churn appear in medium-sized text that provides context without competing for primary attention. Detailed footnotes about methodology appear in small text that's available for those who need it but doesn't distract from the main story.

This hierarchical approach reflects a fundamental principle of progressive disclosure: start with high-level insights and provide mechanisms for viewers to access additional detail as needed. This approach prevents cognitive overload while ensuring that comprehensive information remains available for users who need it. Interactive dashboards exemplify this principle by providing summary views with drill-down capabilities for detailed analysis.

2.4.2 The 60-30-10 Color Rule

Color hierarchy works together with size hierarchy to guide attention and create visual balance. The 60-30-10 rule provides a practical framework for balancing emphasis in data visualizations while maintaining professional appearance and visual coherence.

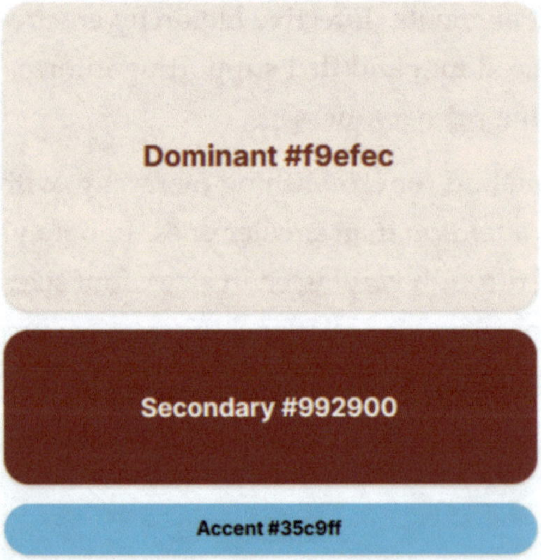

According to this rule, sixty percent of your visual space should use a dominant, neutral color that provides a stable foundation for your design. This might be white or light gray backgrounds, neutral chart areas, or subdued colors for supporting elements. Thirty percent should use a secondary color that complements the dominant color and provides visual interest without overwhelming the design. Ten percent should use an accent color for highlighting the most important elements, such as key data points, call-to-action buttons, or critical insights.

This proportion creates visual balance while ensuring that emphasis remains effective. When everything is highlighted, nothing stands out. The 60-30-10 rule prevents this common mistake by strictly limiting the use of attention-grabbing colors to truly important elements. You can see this principle in action across successful digital products, from mobile apps to professional dashboards.

2.4.3 Creating Balance and Composition

Visual balance creates stability and professionalism in data visualizations while supporting effective information processing. Unlike artistic compositions that might intentionally create tension or imbalance to provoke emotional responses, data visualizations typically benefit from balanced designs that feel stable and trustworthy to viewers.

Symmetrical balance creates formal, stable compositions by distributing visual weight evenly around a central axis. This approach works particularly well for comparative visualizations where equal treatment of different categories or time periods is important. Dashboard layouts often use symmetrical balance to create professional, organized appearances that support systematic information processing.

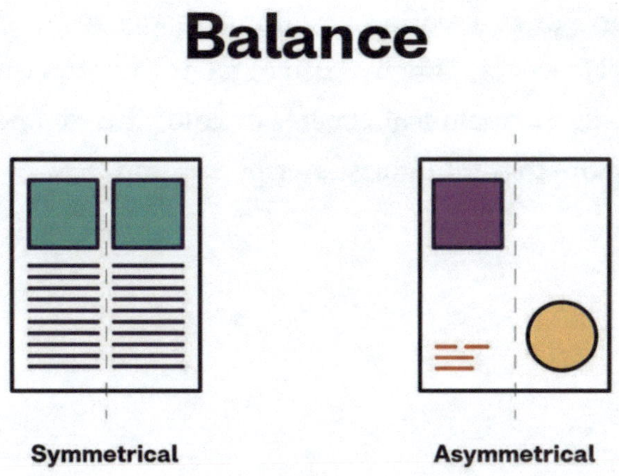

Asymmetrical balance can create more dynamic, engaging compositions while maintaining visual stability. This approach distributes visual weight unevenly but achieves balance through careful consideration of size, color, and positioning. Asymmetrical balance can be particularly effective for storytelling visualizations where you want to create visual interest while guiding viewers through a narrative sequence.

The rule of thirds, borrowed from photography and graphic design, suggests dividing visual space into nine equal sections and placing important elements along the dividing lines or at their intersections. This principle can improve the visual appeal and effectiveness of data visualizations by creating more dynamic, engaging compositions than simple centering.

White space management plays a crucial role in creating balanced, readable visualizations. Adequate white space prevents visual crowding, improves readability, and helps viewers focus on important information. The principle suggests that empty areas are as important as filled areas in creating effective visual communication. Strategic use of white space can group related elements, separate different sections, and provide visual rest areas that prevent cognitive overload.

2.5 Color: Your Most Powerful Tool

2.5.1 Understanding Color Psychology

Color represents one of the most powerful and complex aspects of visual design, capable of conveying information, creating emotional responses, and guiding attention simultaneously. However, effective use of color in data visualization requires understanding both the technical aspects of color theory and the psychological and cultural factors that influence color perception.

Universal color associations exist across many cultures, though these associations are learned rather than innate. Red typically signals urgency, danger, passion, or the instruction to stop. Green commonly represents growth, success, permission to proceed, or connection to nature. Blue conveys trust, stability, calm, and professionalism, which explains its popularity in corporate branding. Yellow demands attention and can suggest caution, optimism, or energy. Gray provides neutrality, professionalism, and sophistication.

However, cultural considerations can override these universal associations in important ways. Red represents good fortune and prosperity in Chinese culture, making it an inappropriate choice for indicating negative values in visualizations intended for Chinese audiences. White symbolizes purity and cleanliness in Western cultures but represents mourning and death in some Asian cultures. These cultural differences underscore the importance of understanding your audience before making color choices.

The psychological impact of color extends beyond conscious associations to influence mood, attention, and decision-making at subconscious levels. Warm colors like red, orange, and yellow tend to advance visually and demand attention, making them effective for highlighting important information. Cool colors like blue, green, and purple tend to recede visually and create calming effects, making them suitable for backgrounds and supporting elements.

2.5.2 Building Effective Color Palettes

Creating professional color palettes requires a systematic approach that balances aesthetic appeal with functional effectiveness. The most successful data visualization color schemes start with a clear understanding of the communication objectives and audience needs, then apply color theory principles to achieve those objectives.

Begin by identifying any existing brand colors that must be incorporated into your design. These colors provide constraints that can improve your design by limiting choices and ensuring consistency with organizational identity. If no brand colors exist, start with a neutral base of grays and off-whites that will provide a stable foundation for your design.

Next, choose one primary accent color that will be used for highlighting the most important information in your visualizations. This color should be sufficiently different from your neutral base to create strong contrast while remaining appropriate for your audience and context. Test this color combination for accessibility compliance before proceeding further.

Add secondary colors only as needed to distinguish between different categories or data series. Each additional color increases cognitive load and reduces the impact of your primary accent color, so use them sparingly. When multiple colors are necessary, choose colors that are sufficiently different from each other to be easily distinguished, even by users with color vision deficiencies.

Professional color tools can streamline this process significantly. Coolors.co generates harmonious color palettes instantly and allows you to lock specific colors while exploring variations. Adobe Color provides more sophisticated color theory tools and integration with professional design software. Contrast checkers ensure that your color combinations meet accessibility standards before you invest time in detailed design work.

2.5.3 Avoiding Common Color Mistakes

Understanding what not to do with color is often as important as understanding best practices. Common color mistakes can undermine even the most carefully planned visualizations and create barriers for users with different abilities or cultural backgrounds.

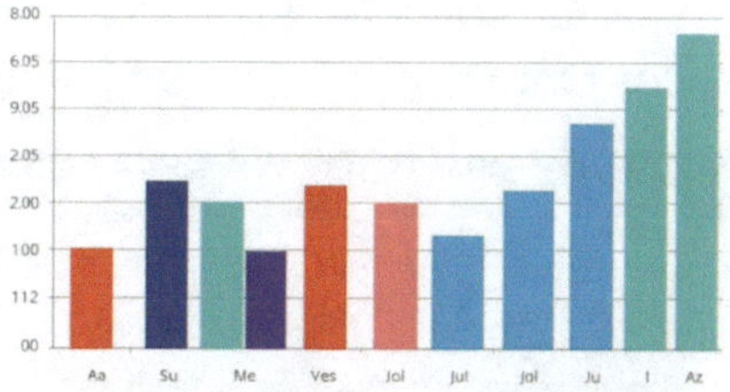

The rainbow chart represents one of the most frequent color mistakes in data visualization. Using every available color creates visual chaos where nothing stands out effectively and viewers struggle to process the information. Limit your color palette to three to five colors maximum, using additional visual elements like patterns or shapes to distinguish between categories when necessary.

Red-green color combinations pose significant accessibility challenges because red-green color blindness is the most common form of color vision deficiency. Always include alternative visual cues like patterns, shapes, or labels when using color to distinguish between categories. This practice benefits all users by providing multiple ways to interpret the information.

Low contrast between text and background colors creates readability problems for all users and violates accessibility standards that are increasingly enforced by law. Test all color combinations using contrast ratio calculators to ensure they meet Web Content Accessibility Guidelines standards before finalizing your design.

Cultural insensitivity in color choices can alienate audiences and undermine your message. Research the cultural context of your audience before making color decisions, particularly when working with international or multicultural groups. When in doubt, choose neutral colors that are less likely to carry unintended cultural meanings.

2.6 Typography: The Unsung Hero

2.6.1 Choosing Fonts That Work

Typography plays a crucial but often underappreciated role in data visualization effectiveness. The fonts you choose can enhance readability and comprehension or create barriers that prevent audiences from accessing your insights. Understanding the principles of effective typography will improve every aspect of your data communications.

Category	Readable Fonts	Problematic Fonts
Sans-serif clarity	Arial	Comic Sans MS
Professional neutrality	Helvetika	Papyrus
Screen legibility	Verdana	Brush Script MT
Data density	Calibri	**Impact**
Print accessibility	Tahoma	Curlz MT

Sans-serif fonts work best for digital data visualizations because they remain readable at small sizes and on various screen types. Arial, Helvetica, and Roboto represent reliable choices that provide clean, simple letterforms with good spacing between characters. These fonts prioritize legibility over personality, which is exactly what data visualization requires.

Avoid decorative fonts that prioritize visual interest over readability. While these fonts might work well for wedding invitations or artistic projects, they create unnecessary cognitive load in data contexts where clarity is paramount. Similarly, avoid using all capital letters for large amounts of text, as this formatting significantly reduces reading speed and comprehension.

Limit yourself to one or two font families per visualization to maintain visual coherence and professional appearance. Using too many different fonts creates a chaotic appearance that undermines credibility and distracts from your data.

When you do use multiple fonts, ensure they complement each other and serve different functional purposes, such as one font for headers and another for body text.

2.6.2 Size and Spacing Guidelines

Proper typography hierarchy guides readers through your visualizations and ensures that important information receives appropriate emphasis. Establishing clear size relationships between different types of text helps viewers understand the relative importance of different elements and navigate complex information efficiently.

Main titles should appear in 24-to-32-point type to establish clear hierarchy and ensure readability from a distance. Section headers work well at 18 to 24 points, providing clear organization without competing with the main title. Body text should range from 12 to 16 points for optimal readability, while captions and footnotes can use 10 to 12 points as long as they remain legible.

Line height, or the vertical space between lines of text, significantly affects readability and should be set to 1.4 to 1.6 times the font size. This spacing provides enough separation between lines to prevent visual crowding while maintaining efficient use of space. Paragraph spacing should equal one line height to create clear separation between different blocks of text.

Margins and padding around text elements should be at least one time the font size to prevent crowding and improve visual hierarchy. These spacing considerations become even more critical for mobile devices, where everything should be approximately twenty percent larger to accommodate smaller screens and touch interfaces.

2.6.3 Typography for Accessibility

Typography accessibility extends beyond basic readability to ensure that your text can be accessed by users with various abilities and assistive technologies. These considerations are not only ethically important but increasingly required by law in many jurisdictions.

Screen readers rely on proper heading structure to help users navigate content efficiently. Use heading tags (H1, H2, H3) in logical order to create a clear information hierarchy that assistive technologies can interpret. Avoid skipping heading levels or using headings purely for visual formatting, as this confuses screen reader users.

Ensure sufficient contrast between text and background colors to meet Web Content Accessibility Guidelines standards. Normal text requires a contrast ratio of at least 4.5 to 1, while large text needs a minimum ratio of 3 to 1. These ratios ensure that users with various visual abilities can read your content comfortably.

Consider how your typography choices will work when users zoom in to 200% magnification, a common accommodation for users with visual impairments. Text should remain readable and functional at this zoom level without requiring horizontal scrolling or losing important information.

2.7 Labels and Formatting: Your Navigation System

2.7.1 Creating Labels That Actually Help

Effective labeling serves as the navigation system for your data visualizations, helping audiences understand what they're seeing and how to interpret it correctly. Poor labeling is one of the most common causes of misinterpretation in data visualization, yet it's also one of the easiest problems to fix with careful attention to clarity and context.

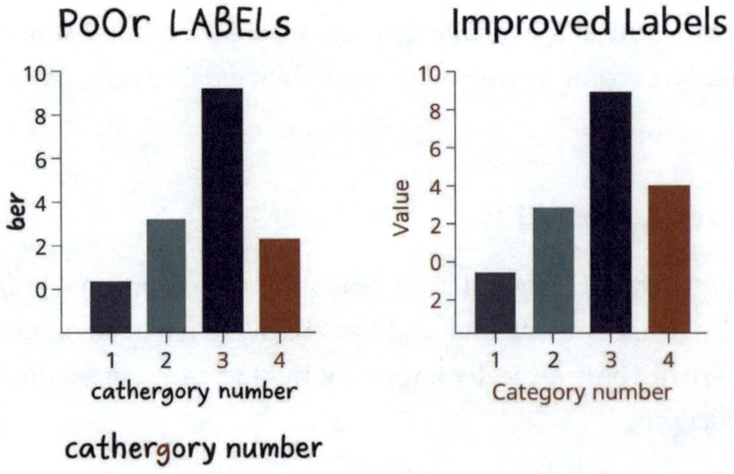

Vague labels like "Q1, Q2, Q3, Q4" leave audiences guessing about which year the data represents and whether the quarters follow a calendar year or fiscal year schedule. Similarly, labels like "Revenue" provide insufficient context about currency, time period, or measurement methodology. "Users" could refer to active users, total users, new users, or any number of other metrics.

Effective labels provide complete context that enables accurate interpretation. "Q1 2024 Revenue (USD Millions)" clearly specifies the time period, currency, and scale. "Monthly Active Users (MAU)" defines exactly what type of user measurement is being presented. "Customer Satisfaction Score (1-10 scale)" explains both what is being measured and how it's measured.

Your labeling checklist should ensure that every visualization includes clear units of measurement, specific time periods, context about what exactly is being measured, and source information about where the data originated. This information might seem obvious to you as the creator, but it's essential for audiences who lack your background knowledge.

2.7.2 Number Formatting for Clarity

How you format numbers significantly affects comprehension and can mean the difference between clear communication and confusion. Consistent, appropriate number formatting reduces cognitive load and helps audiences focus on insights rather than struggling to interpret values.

Use abbreviated formats like "$1.2M" instead of "$1,234,567" when dealing with large numbers, as the abbreviated format is easier to read and compare quickly. Express percentages as "23%" rather than "0.23" to match audience expectations and reduce mental conversion effort. Round numbers appropriately for your context—23.4% tells a clearer story than 23.456789% in most business contexts.

Maintain consistent formatting throughout your visualization to avoid confusion. Don't mix formats like "$1,234" and "$2.3K" in the same chart, as this inconsistency forces viewers to perform mental conversions that distract from your message. Similarly, avoid over-precision that suggests false accuracy—if your underlying data is approximate, your formatting should reflect that reality.

Consider your audience's familiarity with specialized terminology and formatting conventions. Terms like "basis points" or "EBITDA" may be clear to financial professionals but meaningless to general audiences. When specialized terms are necessary, provide clear definitions or use more accessible alternatives.

2.7.3 Progressive Disclosure in Practice

Progressive disclosure represents a fundamental principle of information design that starts with high-level insights and provides mechanisms for accessing additional detail as needed. This approach prevents cognitive overload while ensuring comprehensive information remains available for users who need it.

Google Analytics exemplifies effective progressive disclosure in their reporting interface. The overview dashboard presents total visitors for the current month at the highest level. Users can drill down to see visitors broken down by traffic source, then dive deeper into individual user sessions and behavior patterns. Each level provides appropriate detail for different types of analysis without overwhelming users who only need summary information.

Implement progressive disclosure by designing three levels of information hierarchy. Level one should present high-level summaries that answer the most important questions at a glance. Level two should provide category breakdowns and trend information for users who need more context. Level three should offer detailed data and methodology information for users conducting deep analysis.

Interactive elements like hover states, expandable sections, and drill-down capabilities enable progressive disclosure in digital formats. For static formats, use visual hierarchy and strategic placement to guide viewers from summary information to supporting details in a logical sequence.

2.8 Building Your Design System

2.8.1 Creating Consistency at Scale

A comprehensive design system provides the foundation for consistent, professional data visualizations across projects and team members. Rather than making design decisions from scratch for each visualization, a well-developed system provides tested solutions that ensure quality while improving efficiency.

Your design system (or 'brand kit') should establish a primary color palette of three to five colors that have been tested for accessibility and appropriateness for your audience. Include a secondary palette of neutral grays and supporting colors that complement your primary palette. Document the specific use cases for each color and provide guidance about when and how to use them effectively.

Typography guidelines should specify font families for headers and body text, establish a clear size hierarchy for different types of content, and provide spacing guidelines that ensure consistent, readable layouts. Include guidance about when to use different font weights and styles and specify minimum sizes for different contexts.

Chart type guidelines help team members choose appropriate visualization methods for different types of data and communication objectives. Document when to use bar charts versus line charts, how to handle categorical versus continuous data, and provide templates for common visualization scenarios. Include examples of both effective and problematic implementations to guide decision-making.

2.8.2 Documentation and Implementation

Effective design systems require clear documentation that enables consistent implementation across different team members and projects. This documentation should be accessible, practical, and regularly updated to reflect evolving best practices and organizational needs.

Create a simple style guide template that team members can reference quickly during project work. Include color codes, font specifications, spacing guidelines, and accessibility requirements in an easy-to-scan format. Provide examples of correct implementation alongside common mistakes to prevent misunderstandings.

```
COMPANY DATA VISUALIZATION STYLE GUIDE

COLORS:
Primary: #1f77b4 (Blue) - Use for main data series
Secondary: #ff7f0e (Orange) - Use for comparisons
Neutral: #7f7f7f (Gray) - Use for supporting elements
Background: #ffffff (White) - Standard background

FONTS:
Headers: Roboto Bold, 18-24pt
Body: Roboto Regular, 12-16pt
Captions: Roboto Regular, 10-12pt
Minimum size: 12pt for accessibility

CHARTS:
Bar charts: Use for comparisons between categories
Line charts: Use for trends over time
Pie charts: Avoid - use bar charts instead
Maximum colors per chart: 5

ACCESSIBILITY:
All color combinations tested for 4.5:1 contrast ratio
Patterns or shapes used alongside color coding
Alternative text required for all charts
Keyboard navigation supported for interactive elements
```

Tool recommendations should accommodate different skill levels and budget constraints within your organization. Free options like Canva provide templates and quick design capabilities for basic needs. Professional tools like Adobe Creative Suite or Figma offer advanced features for complex projects. Accessibility testing tools should be integrated into the workflow to ensure compliance with legal requirements.

2.8.3 Maintenance and Evolution

Design systems require ongoing maintenance and evolution to remain effective as technology, best practices, and organizational needs change. Establish regular review cycles to evaluate system effectiveness and identify areas for improvement.

Collect feedback from system users about pain points, missing components, and suggestions for improvement. Track common design mistakes or inconsistencies that suggest gaps in the system documentation. Monitor industry trends and accessibility standards that might require system updates.

Plan for system evolution by building flexibility into your guidelines rather than rigid rules that become obsolete quickly. Focus on principles and frameworks that can adapt to new tools and techniques while maintaining consistency and quality standards.

2.9 Practical Application and Common Pitfalls

2.9.1 Learning from Real-World Success Stories

Examining successful design implementations provides concrete examples of how theoretical principles translate into effective practice. These case studies demonstrate that good design is not about following rules blindly but about applying principles thoughtfully to achieve specific communication objectives.

Spotify's data visualization approach exemplifies effective design system implementation. They maintain consistent brand colors throughout their analytics interfaces while ensuring accessibility compliance. Clear hierarchy using size and contrast guides users through complex listening data without overwhelming them. Progressive disclosure allows users to start with high-level insights about their music preferences and drill down into detailed listening patterns when desired.

The key to Spotify's success lies in their recognition that consistency and accessibility enhance rather than limit creativity. By establishing clear guidelines for color use, typography, and layout, they free their designers to focus on solving communication challenges rather than making basic design decisions repeatedly.

Healthcare dashboard redesigns provide another instructive example of design impact on critical decision-making. A major hospital system transformed their patient monitoring displays by reducing colors from twelve to four, increasing font sizes by twenty percent, adding strategic white space, and implementing comprehensive accessibility standards. The results were dramatic: forty percent faster decision-making by medical staff, sixty percent fewer interpretation errors, and one hundred percent compliance with accessibility regulations.

2.9.2 Avoiding Common Design Mistakes

Understanding frequent design mistakes helps prevent problems that can undermine even well-intentioned visualization efforts. These mistakes often stem from prioritizing visual appeal over functional effectiveness or failing to consider diverse user needs during the design process.

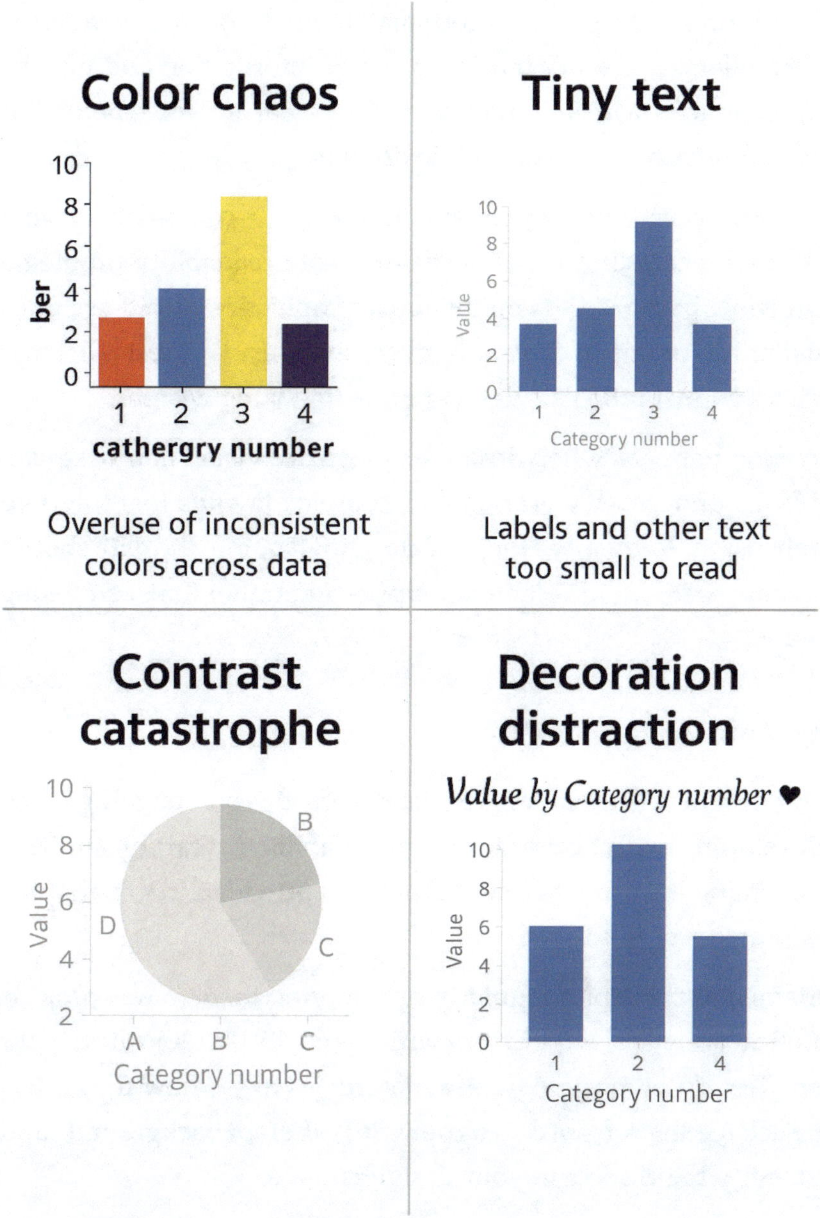

The rainbow explosion mistake involves using every available color in a single visualization, creating visual chaos where nothing stands out effectively. This approach overwhelms viewers and makes it difficult to identify patterns or key insights. The solution is to limit color palettes to maximum three to five colors, using additional visual elements like patterns or shapes when more categories must be distinguished.

Tiny text represents another frequent problem that excludes users and reduces effectiveness for everyone. Labels that are too small to read from a normal viewing distance force audiences to work harder to access information and may violate accessibility standards. Maintain minimum font sizes of twelve points for digital displays and fourteen points for mobile devices.

Contrast catastrophes occur when designers choose color combinations that look appealing but fail accessibility standards or create readability problems. Light gray text on white backgrounds might appear sophisticated but excludes users with visual impairment and strains everyone's eyes. Test all color combinations using contrast ratio calculators before finalizing designs.

Decoration distraction happens when designers prioritize visual flair over clarity, using fancy fonts, unnecessary graphics, or complex layouts that interfere with data comprehension. Remember that in data visualization, the data should be the star of the show, with design elements supporting rather than competing with the information.

2.9.3 Building Your Design Practice

Developing strong design skills requires consistent practice and ongoing learning, much like developing analytical or technical capabilities. Start by auditing your existing work using the principles and checklists provided in this chapter, identifying specific areas for improvement.

Practice the fundamental principles regularly by applying them to real projects rather than theoretical exercises. Experiment with the 60-30-10 color rule in your next presentation. Test different typography hierarchies to see how they affect comprehension. Seek feedback from colleagues with different backgrounds and perspectives to identify blind spots in your design choices.

Stay current with evolving best practices by following design communities, attending workshops, and reading current research on visualization effectiveness. The field of data visualization continues to evolve rapidly, with new tools, techniques, and understanding emerging regularly.

Build accessibility testing into your regular workflow rather than treating it as an optional final step. Use contrast checkers, screen reader testing, and keyboard navigation verification as standard parts of your design process. This proactive approach prevents costly redesigns and ensures that your work serves all potential users effectively.

2.10 The Future of Data Design

2.10.1 Emerging Trends and Technologies

The landscape of data visualization design continues to evolve rapidly, driven by advancing technology, changing user expectations, and growing awareness of accessibility and ethical considerations. Understanding these trends helps prepare you for the future while building skills that will remain relevant as the field develops.

Artificial intelligence is beginning to assist with design decisions, offering suggestions for color palettes, layout optimization, and accessibility improvements. These tools can help democratize good design by providing guidance to users without extensive design training. However, human judgment remains essential for understanding context, audience needs, and communication objectives that AI cannot fully grasp.

Voice interfaces and audio-only interaction represent growing areas of importance as smart speakers and voice assistants become more prevalent. Designing data communications that work effectively in audio-only contexts requires new approaches to information hierarchy and progressive disclosure. This trend also reinforces the importance of clear, descriptive language that works across multiple sensory modalities.

Augmented reality and spatial computing create opportunities for data visualization in three-dimensional space, potentially making complex multidimensional datasets more intuitive to explore. However, these new capabilities also introduce new accessibility challenges and require careful consideration of how spatial design principles apply to data communication.

Personalization and adaptive design allow visualizations to adjust automatically based on user preferences, abilities, and context. This approach could address many accessibility challenges by enabling interfaces that adapt to individual needs rather than requiring users to adapt to fixed designs.

2.10.2 Skills for Future Success

Preparing for the future of data visualization design requires building both technical capabilities and broader design thinking skills that will remain valuable regardless of specific tool changes. Focus on developing a strong foundation in design principles that transcend technologies or trends.

Motion design and animation skills are becoming increasingly important as interactive visualizations become more sophisticated. Understanding how to use motion to guide attention, show transitions, and reveal insights over time will differentiate your work in an increasingly competitive field.

Cross-platform design capabilities ensure that your visualizations work effectively across different devices, screen sizes, and interaction methods. This includes understanding responsive design principles, touch interface considerations, and accessibility requirements for different platforms.

Ethical design awareness helps you navigate the growing recognition that design choices have moral implications. Understanding how visualization design can mislead, exclude, or manipulate audiences will become increasingly important as data visualization plays larger roles in public discourse and decision-making.

User experience research skills enable you to test and validate your design decisions with real users rather than relying solely on design theory or personal preferences. These skills help ensure that your visualizations achieve their intended communication objectives with their intended audiences.

2.11 Conclusion

The tale of two presentations that opened this chapter illustrates a fundamental reality about modern data communication: technical excellence alone is no longer sufficient for professional success. In our increasingly visual world, design competency has become as important as analytical skills for data professionals who want to create meaningful impact.

The principles, techniques, and strategies covered in this chapter provide a comprehensive foundation for effective data visualization design. Visual design basics help you understand how human perception works and how to leverage psychological principles to guide attention and enhance comprehension. Typography and color theory give you the tools to create professional, accessible communications that work for diverse audiences. Accessibility considerations ensure that your work serves all users while often improving the experience for everyone.

Perhaps most importantly, this chapter emphasized that good design is not about decoration or making things look pretty. It's about strategic communication that guides attention to what matters most, reduces cognitive load so people can focus on insights, ensures accessibility so everyone can participate, and builds trust through professional, consistent presentation.

Your design journey starts with your very next visualization. Apply the hierarchy principles to guide viewer attention. Test your color choices for accessibility compliance. Use clear, descriptive labels that provide complete context. Seek feedback from people with different perspectives and abilities. Build these practices into your regular workflow rather than treating them as optional extras.

Remember that design skills, like analytical skills, improve with deliberate practice and ongoing learning. Start with the fundamentals covered in this chapter, then continue developing your capabilities through real projects, feedback from users, and engagement with the broader design community.

The future belongs to data professionals who can combine technical expertise with design competency to create communications that not only inform but inspire action. In a world drowning in data, good design is your life preserver—and your competitive advantage.

Chapter 3

Tools for Data Presentation

3.1 Introduction

Sarah Martinez, a marketing analyst at a mid-sized e-commerce company, faced a familiar challenge on a busy Monday morning. Her CEO needs a comprehensive quarterly performance dashboard by the end of the week, complete with interactive charts showing customer acquisition trends, revenue breakdowns by product category, and predictive forecasts for the next quarter. Two years ago, this request would have sent Sarah into a panic, requiring weeks of coordination with the IT department and expensive consulting fees for custom development.

Instead, Sarah opened her laptop and began working with a suite of modern data presentation tools that would have seemed like science fiction just a few years earlier. Within minutes, she connected her company's sales database to an AI-powered visualization platform that automatically suggested the most effective chart types for her data. A no-code dashboard builder allowed her to create interactive elements without writing a single line of code, while advanced spreadsheet features helped her perform complex calculations and create publication-ready charts.

This transformation represents one of the most significant shifts in the data analytics landscape: the democratization of data visualization through increasingly sophisticated, user-friendly tools. Today's data presentation ecosystem spans from traditional spreadsheet applications enhanced with powerful visualization capabilities to cutting-edge AI platforms that can generate insights and visualizations through natural language commands [1].

The modern data professional must navigate this diverse toolkit strategically, understanding not just how to use individual tools, but when to use them, how to combine them effectively, and how to evaluate new solutions as they emerge. This module provides a comprehensive guide to the current landscape of data presentation tools, from foundational spreadsheet applications to emerging AI-assisted platforms that are reshaping how we create, share, and interact with data visualizations.

3.2 Spreadsheet Tools and Traditional Platforms

3.2.1 Excel

Microsoft Excel remains the most widely used data visualization tool globally, with over 750 million users worldwide as of 2024 [[2]]. Despite being primarily designed as a spreadsheet application, Excel's visualization capabilities have evolved dramatically, making it a formidable platform for data presentation across industries.

Visualization Capabilities

Excel's chart creation engine supports over 20 chart types, from basic column and line charts to advanced statistical visualizations like box plots and histograms. The platform's strength lies in its integration with familiar spreadsheet functionality, allowing users to perform calculations, data manipulation, and visualization within a single environment [[3]].

Recent updates have introduced dynamic arrays, which automatically resize chart ranges as data changes, and enhanced formatting options that rival dedicated visualization software. The introduction of Ideas in Excel leverages machine learning to suggest appropriate chart types and highlight interesting patterns in data, bridging the gap between traditional spreadsheet work and AI-assisted analysis [[4]].

Power BI Integration

The integration between Excel and Microsoft Power BI represents a significant evolution in spreadsheet-based visualization. Users can seamlessly transition from Excel analysis to Power BI dashboards, maintaining data connections and formatting while gaining access to advanced features like real-time data streaming and collaborative sharing [[5]].

This integration addresses one of Excel's traditional limitations: scalability. While Excel excels at individual analysis and small-team collaboration, Power BI extends these capabilities to enterprise-level deployments with thousands of users and massive datasets.

3.2.2 Google Sheets

Google Sheets has emerged as a powerful alternative to Excel, particularly for organizations prioritizing real-time collaboration and cloud-based workflows. The platform's visualization capabilities, while initially limited compared to Excel, have expanded significantly with the introduction of advanced chart types and integration with Google's broader ecosystem [[6]].

Collaborative Advantages

The real-time collaboration features in Google Sheets enable multiple team members to work simultaneously on data analysis and visualization projects. This capability proves particularly valuable for distributed teams and organizations with complex approval processes, where stakeholders need to review and modify visualizations collaboratively [[7]].

Integration Ecosystem

Google Sheets' integration with Google Analytics, Google Ads, and other Google Workspace applications creates a seamless workflow for marketing and business analytics. The platform's ability to automatically refresh data from these sources ensures that visualizations remain current without manual intervention.

3.2.3 Specialized Spreadsheet Solutions

Beyond the dominant Excel and Google Sheets platforms, specialized spreadsheet solutions offer unique advantages for specific use cases. Airtable combines spreadsheet functionality with database capabilities, enabling more sophisticated data relationships and visualization options. Numbers, Apple's spreadsheet application, emphasizes visual design and presentation quality, making it particularly suitable for client-facing reports and presentations [[8]].

3.3 No-Code Platforms

3.3.1 Breaking Down Technical Barriers

The emergence of no-code data visualization platforms represents a fundamental shift in who can create sophisticated data presentations. These tools eliminate the need for programming knowledge, SQL expertise, or advanced technical skills, enabling business users, marketers, and domain experts to create professional-quality visualizations independently [[9]].

Tableau

Tableau pioneered the drag-and-drop approach to data visualization, introducing concepts that have become standard across the industry. The platform's visual query language allows users to explore data intuitively, building complex analyses through simple interactions rather than code [[10]].

Recent developments in Tableau include enhanced natural language processing capabilities, allowing users to ask questions about their data in plain English and receive appropriate visualizations. The platform's AI-powered features can automatically detect interesting patterns and suggest relevant analyses, reducing the time from data to insight [[11]].

Looker Studio: Google's Answer

Google's Looker Studio (formerly Data Studio) provides free access to professional-grade data visualization capabilities, democratizing access to tools that were previously expensive and complex. The platform's strength lies in its seamless integration with Google's advertising and analytics ecosystem, making it particularly valuable for digital marketing professionals [[12]].

Power BI

Microsoft Power BI combines the accessibility of no-code design with enterprise-grade security and scalability. The platform's integration with Microsoft's broader ecosystem, including Office 365 and Azure, creates a comprehensive business intelligence solution that scales from individual users to large organizations [[13]].

3.3.2 Emerging No-Code Platforms

Datylon

Datylon represents a new generation of no-code platforms that prioritize design quality and brand consistency. The platform enables users to create charts and reports that maintain consistent branding and professional appearance across different outputs [[14]].

Flourish

Flourish specializes in creating interactive, animated visualizations that engage audiences through storytelling. The platform's template-based approach allows users to create sophisticated animations and interactive elements without technical expertise, making it particularly valuable for journalism, marketing, and educational content [[15]].

3.3.3 Democratization

The democratization of data visualization through no-code platforms has profound implications for organizational decision-making. Research indicates that organizations with widespread access to self-service analytics tools make decisions 5 times faster than those relying on centralized IT departments for visualization creation [[16]].

However, this democratization also introduces new challenges. Without proper governance and training, organizations risk creating inconsistent, misleading, or poorly designed visualizations. The most successful implementations combine accessible tools with comprehensive training programs and clear design guidelines [[17]].

3.4 The AI Revolution

3.4.1 Natural Language Interfaces

The integration of artificial intelligence into data visualization tools represents the next frontier in accessibility and efficiency. AI-powered platforms can interpret natural language queries, automatically select appropriate visualization types, and even generate insights from data without explicit user direction [[18]].

ThoughtSpot: Conversational Analytics

ThoughtSpot's search-driven approach allows users to query data using natural language, receiving immediate visualizations and insights. The platform's AI engine, Spotter, can automatically detect anomalies, trends, and correlations, presenting findings in easily digestible formats [[19]].

Recent developments include AI agents that can proactively monitor data and alert users to significant changes or opportunities. This shift from reactive to proactive analytics represents a fundamental change in how organizations interact with their data [[20]].

Julius AI: Conversational Data Analysis

Julius AI exemplifies the new generation of AI-powered visualization tools that combine natural language processing with automated chart generation. Users can upload datasets and ask questions in plain English, receiving both visualizations and analytical insights without needing to understand underlying statistical concepts [[21]].

3.4.2 Automated Design Intelligence

AI-assisted design goes beyond simple chart generation to include sophisticated design decisions that traditionally required human expertise. Modern AI tools can automatically select color palettes that ensure accessibility compliance, choose appropriate chart types based on data characteristics, and optimize layouts for different display formats [[22]].

Polymer: AI-Driven Insights

Polymer uses machine learning to automatically identify patterns, outliers, and relationships in data, presenting findings through interactive dashboards that require no setup or configuration. The platform's AI can generate natural language explanations of trends and anomalies, making complex data accessible to non-technical users [[23]].

Zoho Analytics: Zia AI Assistant

Zoho Analytics integrates Zia, an AI assistant that can answer questions about data, suggest visualizations, and even predict future trends based on historical patterns. This integration of predictive analytics with visualization creation enables users to create forward-looking dashboards and reports [[24]].

3.4.3 The Future of AI in Visualization

Emerging AI capabilities include automated data cleaning and preparation, intelligent data source integration, and predictive visualization that anticipates user needs. These developments promise to further reduce the time and expertise required to create meaningful data presentations while improving the quality and relevance of insights generated [[25]].

3.5 Tool Selection Framework

3.5.1 Assessment Criteria

Selecting the appropriate data presentation tool requires systematic evaluation across multiple dimensions. The most effective approach involves assessing tools against specific organizational needs, technical constraints, and strategic objectives rather than pursuing a one-size-fits-all solution.

Technical Requirements

When evaluating data presentation tools, it's essential to consider several technical requirements that influence their effectiveness and suitability. First, the tool's ability to manage data volume and complexity plays a critical role, as some platforms are better equipped to handle large datasets, perform intricate calculations, and process real-time data streams. Integration capabilities are equally important, ensuring that the tool can seamlessly connect with existing data sources, databases, and business applications to maintain workflow continuity. Performance and speed also factor heavily into the decision, as fast response times for data processing, visualization rendering, and user interactions contribute to a smoother user experience. Lastly, security and compliance must be prioritized, with robust data protection features, granular user access controls, and adherence to relevant regulatory standards forming the backbone of a trustworthy and compliant data environment. [[26]]

User Experience Factors

User experience plays a pivotal role in the effectiveness of data presentation tools, influencing adoption, productivity, and collaboration. One key factor is the learning curve, which refers to the time and effort required for users to become proficient with the tool. A steep learning curve can hinder widespread usage, while intuitive interfaces promote faster onboarding. Collaboration features are also essential, enabling real-time sharing, commenting, version control, and multi-user editing that support teamwork and streamline feedback loops. Mobile accessibility is increasingly important, as users expect high-quality interfaces and offline functionality across devices to maintain productivity on the go. Finally, customization options allow organizations to tailor visualizations to their brand identity, modify appearances, and create custom chart types that better communicate insights and maintain consistency across outputs. [[27]]

Business Considerations

Business considerations are a crucial dimension when selecting a data presentation tool, as they directly impact long-term sustainability and organizational success. The total cost of ownership must be carefully assessed, not only licensing fees but also implementation costs, training expenses, and ongoing maintenance requirements. Scalability is another key factor, ensuring that the tool can expand alongside organizational growth and accommodate an increasing user base without compromising performance. Vendor stability plays an important role as well, since the long-term viability of the platform and the quality of customer support can determine whether the investment remains reliable over time. Finally, strategic alignment ensures that the chosen tool integrates seamlessly with the existing technology stack and supports the organization's future direction, reinforcing both operational efficiency and strategic objectives. [[28]]

3.5.2 Decision Matrix Approach

A structured decision matrix helps organizations evaluate tools objectively across these criteria. Weigh each factor according to organizational priorities, score each tool against the criteria, and calculate overall rankings to guide selection decisions.

3.6 Integration and Workflow Strategies

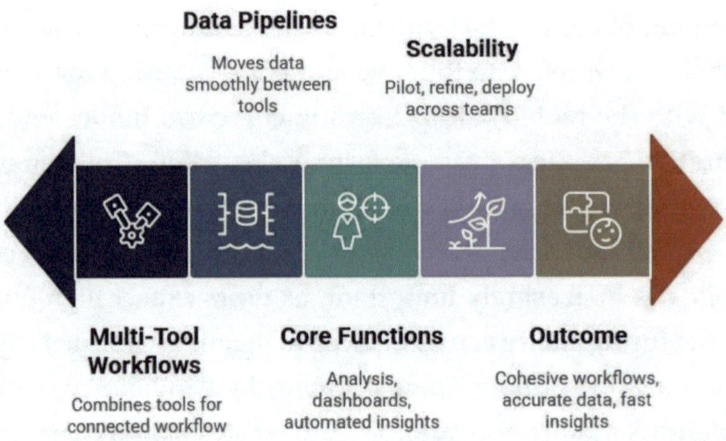

Modern organizations rarely rely on a single data tool. Instead, they use multiple tools together in connected workflows, with each tool performing a specific role. For example, spreadsheets like Excel or Google Sheets are often used for initial data exploration, calculations, and hypothesis testing. No-code platforms such as Tableau or Power BI are then used to create interactive dashboards for stakeholders, while AI-powered tools can automatically identify trends, generate insights, or even produce preliminary visualizations. Specialized tools, like geographic mapping software or statistical analysis platforms, may also be integrated for needs. By using multiple tools this way, organizations can leverage the strengths of each platform while keeping data consistent and workflows efficient.

To make these hybrid workflows effective, organizations establish data pipelines that move information smoothly between tools. Data pipelines ensure that dashboards, reports, and AI analyses are all working with the same up-to-date data. Automation tools such as Zapier, Microsoft Power Automate, or custom scripts can synchronize data across platforms, reducing manual entry, minimizing errors, and saving time. Integrated workflows often include triggers and scheduled processes, such as automatically updating dashboards when data changes, distributing reports to relevant stakeholders on a fixed schedule, and maintaining version control across different tools.

These connected workflows allow organizations to support three main functions: analysis, dashboards, and automated insights. Analysis happens in spreadsheets or statistical software, dashboards communicate key information to decision-makers, and AI-powered tools or specialized platforms provide automated insights that highlight trends, anomalies, or opportunities without requiring manual review. By combining these functions into a single, coordinated workflow, teams can work faster, maintain accuracy, and respond more effectively to changing business conditions.

Furthermore, integrated workflows are scalable and flexible. Organizations can pilot new tools in small projects, gather feedback from users, and then deploy successful tools across departments. Training programs and clear governance standards, including data quality rules and design consistency, help ensure that multiple tools work together effectively and that users adopt them successfully. Over time, these workflows can evolve to incorporate emerging trends such as real-time data updates, augmented analytics platforms, or AI-assisted decision-making, further improving efficiency and insight generation.

By combining multiple tools, establishing data pipelines, automating key processes, and maintaining governance and training, organizations create cohesive workflows that support analysis, dashboards, and automated insights in a consistent, efficient, and scalable way. This structured approach ensures that data is accurate, visualizations are meaningful, and insights are delivered quickly to the people who need them.

3.7 Conclusion

The landscape of data presentation tools has undergone a remarkable transformation. From the early days when creating a comprehensive dashboard required weeks of coordination and specialized technical knowledge, today's professionals can leverage a vast ecosystem of tools that make sophisticated analysis accessible to almost anyone. Traditional spreadsheet applications like Excel and Google Sheets continue to serve as powerful foundations, offering familiarity, flexibility, and integration with enterprise systems. Meanwhile, no-code platforms such as Tableau, Power BI, and Looker Studio have lowered barriers further, enabling business users to produce interactive, publication-quality visualizations without programming expertise.

At the same time, AI-powered tools are redefining what is possible, allowing natural language queries, automated insight generation, and predictive analysis that would have been unimaginable just a few years ago. These technologies not only accelerate workflows but also enhance the quality and relevance of insights, transforming data from static tables into actionable knowledge that drives faster, more informed decision-making.

However, the proliferation of tools also introduces complexity. Success in this environment requires more than technical proficiency, demands strategic evaluation of each platform's capabilities, careful integration into existing workflows, and consistent governance to ensure accuracy, clarity, and design consistency. Organizations that combine multiple tools into connected workflows, automate key processes, and invest in training and best practices can harness the full potential of modern data presentation, creating dashboards that communicate effectively, analyses that inform decisively, and AI-generated insights that anticipate opportunities.

Ultimately, the democratization of data visualization represents a cultural as well as technological shift. Modern data professionals are no longer just creators of charts; they are orchestrators of an ecosystem that turns raw data into strategic assets. By understanding the strengths and limitations of each tool, integrating them effectively, and leveraging emerging AI capabilities, organizations can unlock faster, more insightful, and more impactful decision-making—ensuring that data becomes not just a record of the past, but a guide to the future.

Chapter 4

Accessibility and Usability

4.1 Introduction

Dr. Elena Rodriguez thought she had created the perfect COVID-19 vaccination dashboard. The interactive map displayed vaccination rates across her state in vibrant blues and greens, with hover-over details revealing precise statistics for each county. The color-coded legend made patterns immediately obvious—or so she believed. Red counties needed urgent attention, yellow counties showed moderate progress, and green counties had achieved target vaccination rates.

She was preparing to present this dashboard to a coalition of government officials, community leaders, and disability advocates when her colleague Marcus asked to review her work. Marcus, who had lost his vision in a car accident five years earlier, relied on screen reader software to navigate digital content. Elena watched as he opened her dashboard and began exploring.

After several minutes of frustrated clicking and navigation attempts, Marcus looked up with a gentle but firm expression. "Elena, this is clearly important data," he said, "but it's completely invisible to me. Your beautiful visualization excludes not just me, but millions of people who need this health information most."

That moment changed everything for Elena. She realized that her stunning visualization, despite containing crucial public health data, was fundamentally inaccessible to a significant portion of the population it was meant to serve. The very people who might be most vulnerable to COVID-19—including many in the disability community—couldn't access the information designed to protect them.

Elena's experience illustrates a fundamental challenge in modern data communication: the tension between creating visually compelling presentations and ensuring universal accessibility. This chapter explores how to resolve that tension, demonstrating that accessibility isn't a constraint on good design but rather a catalyst for better, more inclusive communication.

4.2 The Imperative for Inclusive Design

4.2.1 Understanding the Scope of Accessibility Needs

The case for accessible data visualization extends far beyond legal compliance or ethical considerations, though both are compelling. When Elena began researching accessibility after her encounter with Marcus, she discovered that approximately 1.3 billion people worldwide live with some form of disability . In the United States alone, this represents about 26% of adults—roughly one in four people . These aren't abstract statistics; they represent colleagues, family members, community leaders, and decision-makers who need access to data to make informed choices about their lives and work.

The scope of accessibility challenges in data visualization is broader than many people realize. Color blindness affects approximately 8% of men and 0.5% of women, meaning that visualizations relying solely on color to convey information immediately exclude millions of users. Visual impairments range from complete blindness to low vision conditions that make small text or low-contrast elements difficult or impossible to read. Motor disabilities can make precise mouse movements challenging, while cognitive disabilities may affect how people process complex visual information.

But accessibility challenges extend beyond permanent disabilities. Situational limitations affect everyone at various times. Try reading a colorful chart on your phone in bright sunlight, and you'll experience what low vision users face daily. Attempt to navigate a complex dashboard while holding a baby, and you'll understand the importance of keyboard accessibility. These temporary limitations remind us that accessible design benefits everyone, not just people with permanent disabilities.

4.2.2 The Legal and Business Landscape

The legal landscape surrounding digital accessibility has evolved rapidly in recent years. The Americans with Disabilities Act, originally passed in 1990, has been increasingly applied to digital content through court decisions and regulatory guidance. In 2024, the U.S. Department of Justice finalized comprehensive accessibility rules for government websites , while the European Union's Accessibility Act came into full effect in 2025 . Organizations that ignore accessibility face real legal consequences, with thousands of accessibility-related lawsuits filed annually.

The financial implications of inaccessible design extend beyond legal costs. Target Corporation paid $6 million to settle an accessibility lawsuit in 2006, while Domino's Pizza faced years of litigation over their inaccessible website and mobile app. These cases established important precedents and demonstrated that accessibility isn't just a nice-to-have feature—it's a legal requirement with real financial consequences.

Beyond legal requirements, the business case for accessibility is compelling. When Elena eventually redesigned her dashboard with accessibility in mind, she discovered that the improvements benefited all users. Better color contrast made the visualization easier to read in various lighting conditions. Clear, descriptive labels reduced confusion for everyone. Keyboard navigation proved useful for power users who preferred shortcuts to mouse clicking. The accessible version wasn't just compliant—it was better.

4.2.3 The Hidden Costs of Inaccessible Design

Elena's research revealed that inaccessible design creates hidden costs that organizations often don't recognize. Customer service departments field more calls when websites and applications are difficult to use. Training costs increase when interfaces are confusing or inconsistent. Employee productivity suffers when internal tools exclude team members with disabilities.

Consider the case of a major financial services company that discovered their quarterly earnings dashboard was inaccessible to several key stakeholders, including a board member with low vision and analysts who relied on screen readers. The company had to create alternative formats for each quarterly report, a time-consuming process that delayed decision-making and created additional work for multiple departments. When they eventually redesigned the dashboard with accessibility in mind, they eliminated these workarounds while improving the experience for all users.

4.3 Understanding WCAG: The Foundation of Digital Accessibility

4.3.1 The POUR Principles in Practice

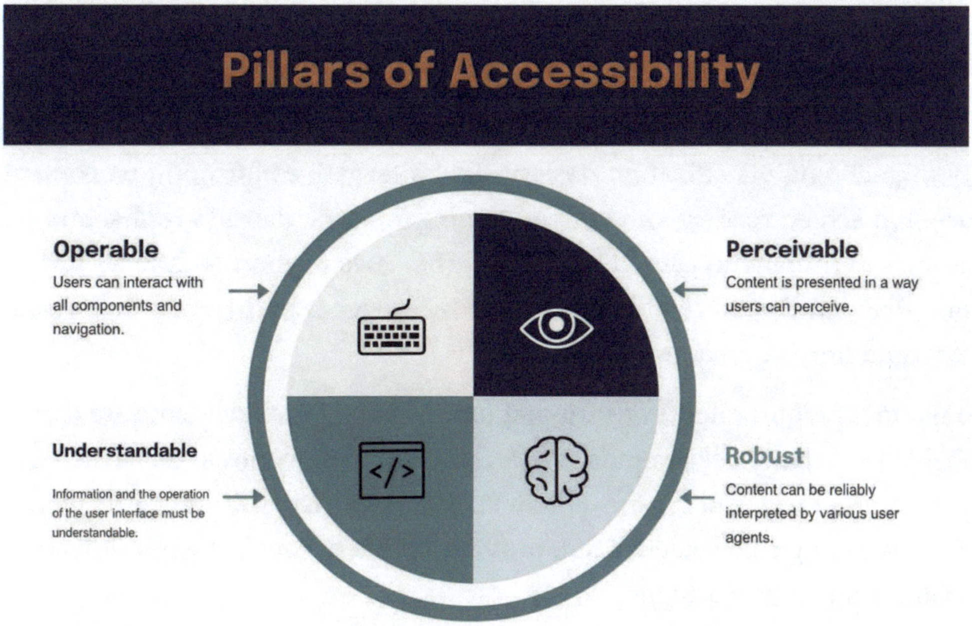

The Web Content Accessibility Guidelines, known as WCAG, provide the international standard for digital accessibility . Think of WCAG as building codes for the digital world—just as physical structures must meet safety standards to protect occupants, digital content must meet accessibility standards to ensure universal access.

WCAG 2.2, released in December 2023, represents the current standard that most accessibility laws reference. The guidelines are built around four fundamental principles, remembered by the acronym POUR: Perceivable, Operable, Understandable, and Robust. These principles provide a framework for thinking about accessibility that extends beyond specific technical requirements.

The Perceivable principle requires that information be presentable in ways users can perceive, regardless of their sensory abilities. For data visualizations, this means ensuring that information isn't conveyed through color alone, that text has sufficient contrast against backgrounds, and that complex graphics have alternative text descriptions. When Elena's original dashboard used only color to indicate vaccination rates, it violated this principle by making the information imperceptible to users who couldn't distinguish between the colors.

4.3.2 Perceivable: Making Information Accessible to All Senses

The Perceivable principle encompasses several specific requirements that directly impact data visualization design. Text alternatives for non-text content ensure that screen readers can convey the meaning of charts, graphs, and infographics to users who cannot see them. This goes beyond simple alt text to include detailed descriptions that capture the insights and trends that visual users would immediately recognize.

Color contrast requirements ensure that text and graphical elements are distinguishable from their backgrounds. WCAG 2.2 requires a contrast ratio of at least 4.5:1 for normal text and 3:1 for large text. For data visualizations, this means carefully selecting color palettes that provide sufficient contrast while still creating visually appealing designs.

Resizable text requirements ensure that users can increase text size up to 200% without losing functionality or content. This particularly impacts data visualizations that include labels, legends, and annotations. Elena discovered that her original dashboard broke when users increased text size, with labels overlapping and becoming unreadable. Her redesigned version used responsive design techniques to accommodate various text sizes gracefully.

4.3.3 Operable: Ensuring Universal Interaction

The Operable principle demands that interface components work for all users, including those using assistive technologies. This encompasses keyboard navigation, ensuring that interactive elements can be activated without a mouse, and avoiding content that flashes rapidly enough to trigger seizures. Elena's dashboard initially failed this test because its hover-over functionality only worked with mouse interaction, making detailed data inaccessible to keyboard users.

Keyboard accessibility requires that all functionality be available through keyboard navigation. This means providing logical tab order, visible focus indicators, and keyboard shortcuts for complex interactions. Elena's redesigned dashboard allowed users to navigate through data points using arrow keys, activate detailed views with the Enter key, and access help information with designated function keys.

Timing considerations ensure that users have adequate time to read and interact with content. Auto-updating dashboards can be problematic for users who need more time to process information or who use assistive technologies that read content aloud. Elena's accessible dashboard included controls to pause automatic updates and extend time limits when necessary.

4.3.4 Understandable: Clarity in Communication and Interface

The Understandable principle requires that information and interface operation be comprehensible to users. This involves using clear language, organizing content logically, and providing helpful error messages when things go wrong. For data visualizations, this might mean explaining technical terms, providing context for statistical measures, or offering guidance on how to interpret complex charts.

Readable text goes beyond basic literacy to consider cognitive load and comprehension. Elena learned to write alternative text that not only described what a chart showed but also explained what it meant. Instead of simply stating "Bar chart showing vaccination rates by county," her descriptions included context: "Bar chart showing vaccination rates by county, with most counties achieving 60-70% vaccination rates but three counties falling below 50%, indicating need for targeted outreach efforts."

Predictable functionality ensures that interface elements behave consistently throughout an application. When Elena standardized the interaction patterns across her dashboard—making all data points respond to the same keyboard shortcuts and providing consistent feedback for user actions—she reduced cognitive load for all users while making the interface more accessible to people with cognitive disabilities.

4.3.5 Robust: Future-Proofing Accessibility

The Robust principle ensures that content works with various assistive technologies, both current and future. This typically involves using standard HTML markup and following established coding practices that assistive technologies can reliably interpret.

Semantic markup provides meaning and structure that assistive technologies can understand. Elena learned to use proper heading hierarchies, table structures, and form labels that screen readers could interpret correctly. This semantic foundation made her visualizations accessible not just to current assistive technologies but also to future innovations in accessibility tools.

Valid code ensures that content renders correctly across different browsers and assistive technologies. Elena incorporated code validation into her development process, catching errors that might cause accessibility problems before they reached users.

4.3.6 WCAG Conformance Levels and Practical Implementation

WCAG defines three levels of conformance: A, AA, and AAA. Level A addresses the most basic accessibility features and removes the most significant barriers. Level AA, which most organizations target, provides a reasonable level of accessibility for most users and is required by most accessibility laws. Level AAA represents the highest level of accessibility but is often impractical to achieve for entire websites or applications.

For data visualization, Level AA compliance typically means ensuring color contrast ratios of at least 4.5:1 for normal text and 3:1 for large text, providing alternative text for images and charts, ensuring keyboard accessibility, and organizing content with proper headings. These requirements might seem technical, but they translate into practical design decisions that improve the experience for all users.

Elena discovered that achieving Level AA compliance wasn't as restrictive as she initially feared. The guidelines provided a framework for making design decisions that improved usability for everyone. Better contrast made her visualizations easier to read in various lighting conditions. Proper heading structure made complex dashboards easier to navigate. Keyboard accessibility proved popular with power users who preferred shortcuts to mouse navigation.

4.4 Making Data Visualizations Accessible

4.4.1 Color, Contrast, and Alternative Text

The process of creating accessible data visualizations begins with understanding how different users might interact with your content. Screen reader users navigate through content sequentially, hearing text read aloud and relying on proper markup to understand structure and relationships. Users with motor disabilities might navigate entirely with a keyboard, using tab keys to move between interactive elements. People with cognitive disabilities benefit from clear, consistent layouts and plain language explanations.

Color presents one of the most common accessibility challenges in data visualization. Elena's original dashboard used red, yellow, and green to indicate vaccination progress—a logical choice that aligned with common traffic light metaphors. However, red-green color blindness is the most common form of color vision deficiency, making this color scheme problematic for many users. The solution isn't to avoid color entirely but to ensure that color isn't the only way information is conveyed.

4.4.2 Designing with Color Accessibility in Mind

Effective accessible design uses multiple visual cues to communicate information. Instead of relying solely on red and green, Elena's redesigned dashboard used patterns, shapes, and direct labeling. Counties with low vaccination rates were shown in red with diagonal stripes and labeled "Below Target." Counties meeting goals appeared in green with solid fill and "Target Met" labels. This approach made the information accessible to users with color vision deficiencies while remaining clear for all users.

The selection of accessible color palettes requires careful consideration of different types of color vision deficiency. Protanopia affects red perception, deuteranopia affects green perception, and tritanopia affects blue perception. Elena used color blindness simulation tools to test her visualizations from the perspective of users with different types of color vision deficiency, ensuring that her color choices remained distinguishable across all conditions.

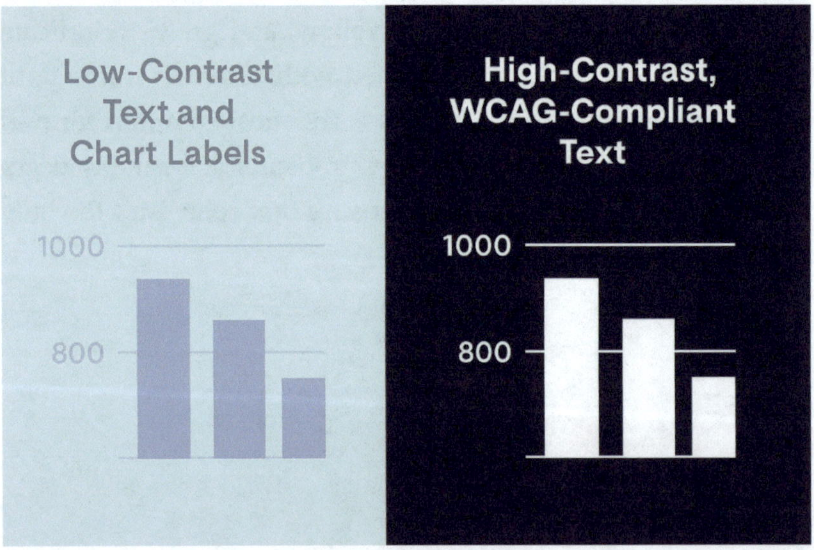

Contrast is another critical consideration. WCAG requires a contrast ratio of at least 4.5:1 between text and background colors for normal-sized text, and 3:1 for large text. These ratios ensure that text remains readable for users with low vision or in challenging viewing conditions. Many designers initially worry that these requirements will limit their creative options, but in practice, good contrast improves readability for everyone and often results in cleaner, more professional-looking designs.

Elena discovered that achieving proper contrast often led to better design decisions. High-contrast color schemes forced her to be more intentional about which elements to emphasize, resulting in cleaner, more focused visualizations. She learned to use online contrast checkers during the design process, testing color combinations before committing to them in her final designs.

4.4.3 Crafting Effective Alternative Text

Alternative text for charts and graphs requires careful consideration of what information is most important to convey. A simple bar chart showing quarterly sales might have alternative text like: "Bar chart showing quarterly sales for 2024. Sales increased steadily from $2.1 million in Q1 to $2.4 million in Q4, representing 14% growth over the year." This description provides both the chart type and the key insight, allowing screen reader users to understand the main message without seeing the visual representation.

Elena developed a systematic approach to writing alternative text that captured both the literal content and the intended insights of her visualizations. She started with the chart type and data source, then described the main trends or patterns, and concluded with the key takeaway or implication. For complex visualizations, she provided multiple levels of description: a brief summary for quick understanding and detailed descriptions for users who needed comprehensive information.

The challenge of alternative text becomes more complex with interactive visualizations. Elena learned to provide both static descriptions of the overall visualization and dynamic descriptions that updated as users interacted with different elements. Her COVID-19 dashboard included a summary description of the overall state vaccination picture, plus detailed descriptions that appeared when users focused on specific counties or data points.

4.4.4 Data Tables as Universal Alternatives

For complex visualizations, alternative text alone may not be sufficient. Data tables provide a comprehensive alternative that allows screen reader users to explore data in detail. Elena's dashboard included a data table showing vaccination rates for each county, organized alphabetically with clear column headers.

Users could sort by vaccination rate, population, or geographic region to find the information most relevant to their needs.

Proper table structure is crucial for accessibility. Elena learned to use table headers (`<th>` elements) to identify column and row labels, table captions to provide context, and summary attributes to explain the table's purpose and organization. She also ensured that complex tables included scope attributes to clarify whether headers applied to columns, rows, or groups of cells.

Vaccination Rates by County

County	Population	Vaccination Rate
Adams	50,000	72%
Baker	120,000	65%
Clark	80,000	81%

```
<table
  role=table" aria-label="
Vaccination Rates by County"
summary="This table lists cou-
nties alphabetically with
population and vaccination
rate.">
<caption>
  Vaccination Rates by County
  <thead>
    <th scope="col<County>
    <th scope="col=Populationn>
    <th scope="col=Vaccination
      Rate;">
    </tbody>
    <tr>=
    <td?=
  </table>
</table>
```

The relationship between visualizations and their corresponding data tables requires careful consideration. Elena positioned data tables immediately after their corresponding visualizations, with clear headings that linked the two presentations of the same information. She also provided navigation shortcuts that allowed users to jump between the visual and tabular representations of the data.

4.4.5 Interactive Accessibility Considerations

Interactive elements in data visualizations must work for users who can't use a mouse. This means ensuring that all functionality is available through keyboard navigation, that focus indicators clearly show which element is currently selected, and that interactive elements are large enough to activate easily. Elena's redesigned dashboard allowed users to tab through counties on the map, press Enter to view detailed information, and use arrow keys to navigate through data points.

Touch target size becomes critical for users with motor disabilities and for mobile accessibility. WCAG guidelines recommend that interactive elements be at least 44 by 44 pixels, roughly the size of an adult fingertip. Elena ensured that all clickable elements in her dashboard met this requirement, with adequate spacing between adjacent interactive elements to prevent accidental activation.

Focus management in complex interactive visualizations requires careful planning. Elena implemented a logical focus order that followed the visual layout of her dashboard, with clear focus indicators that remained visible against all background colors. She also provided skip links that allowed keyboard users to bypass repetitive navigation and jump directly to main content areas.

4.5 Beyond Visual Disabilities: Cognitive and Motor Accessibility

4.5.1 Designing for Cognitive Accessibility

While visual accessibility often receives the most attention, cognitive and motor accessibility are equally important for creating truly inclusive data visualizations. Cognitive disabilities affect how people process information, while motor disabilities impact how they interact with digital interfaces. Designing for these needs often results in improvements that benefit all users.

Cognitive accessibility focuses on making information clear and understandable.

This involves using plain language, organizing content logically, and avoiding unnecessary complexity. For data visualizations, cognitive accessibility might mean providing clear titles and labels, explaining technical terms, and presenting information in a logical sequence. Elena discovered that when she simplified the language in her dashboard and added brief explanations of key terms like "vaccination rate" and "herd immunity threshold," the visualization became more useful for everyone, not just users with cognitive disabilities.

4.5.2 Progressive Disclosure and Information Architecture

Progressive disclosure is a powerful technique for cognitive accessibility. Instead of presenting all available data at once, progressive disclosure starts with high-level insights and allows users to drill down for more detail. Elena's redesigned dashboard initially showed state-level vaccination progress, then allowed users to explore regional and county-level data. This approach prevented cognitive overload while still providing access to detailed information for users who needed it.

The information architecture of data visualizations significantly impacts cognitive accessibility. Elena learned to organize information hierarchically, with clear headings and logical groupings that helped users understand the structure and relationships within the data. She used consistent navigation patterns throughout her dashboard, reducing the cognitive load required to learn new interaction methods.

Error prevention and recovery became important considerations in Elena's accessible design process. She implemented input validation that prevented users from making mistakes, clear error messages that explained what went wrong and how to fix it, and confirmation dialogs for destructive actions. These features particularly benefited users with cognitive disabilities but improved the experience for all users.

4.5.3 Consistency and Predictability

Consistency in design and interaction patterns reduces cognitive load by allowing users to predict how elements will behave. When Elena ensured that all interactive elements in her dashboard responded to the same keyboard shortcuts and followed the same visual patterns, users could focus on understanding the data rather than learning new interface conventions.

Visual consistency extends beyond interaction patterns to include consistent use of colors, fonts, and layout principles. Elena developed a design system for her dashboard that specified how different types of information should be presented, ensuring that users could quickly recognize and understand different elements based on their visual treatment.

Predictable behavior in interactive elements helps users build mental models of how the interface works. Elena ensured that similar-looking elements behaved similarly, that actions had consistent results, and that the interface provided clear feedback for all user interactions.

4.5.4 Motor Accessibility and Interaction Design

Motor accessibility considerations include ensuring that interactive elements are large enough to activate easily, providing adequate spacing between clickable areas, and offering alternatives to complex gestures. The WCAG guidelines recommend that touch targets be at least 44 by 44 pixels, roughly the size of an adult fingertip. This requirement benefits not only users with motor disabilities but also anyone using a mobile device or working in challenging conditions.

Keyboard navigation is essential for users who cannot use a mouse due to motor disabilities. This means ensuring that all interactive functionality is available through keyboard shortcuts, that the tab order follows a logical sequence, and that users can see which element currently has focus. Elena's dashboard allowed users to navigate through all interactive elements using only the Tab, Enter, and arrow keys, making it accessible to users with various motor limitations.

4.5.5 Alternative Input Methods and Assistive Technologies

Elena learned about various assistive technologies that users with motor disabilities employ to interact with digital content. Switch navigation allows users with limited mobility to navigate interfaces using one or two switches, often activated by head movement, eye blinks, or breath control. Voice recognition software enables users to control computers through spoken commands. Eye-tracking systems allow users to navigate and activate interface elements by looking at them.

Designing for these alternative input methods requires understanding their capabilities and limitations. Switch navigation typically requires simplified interfaces with clear focus indicators and logical tab order. Voice recognition works best with interfaces that have consistent, predictable labels and commands. Eye-tracking systems need adequate spacing between interactive elements and clear visual feedback.

Elena incorporated support for these technologies by following standard web accessibility practices: using semantic HTML markup, providing proper labels for all interactive elements, and ensuring that her dashboard worked well with keyboard navigation. These foundational practices made her visualizations compatible with most assistive technologies without requiring specialized coding.

4.5.6 Timing and Motion Considerations

Time limits can create barriers for users who need more time to process information or interact with interfaces. Elena's original dashboard automatically refreshed data every few minutes, potentially disrupting users who were in the middle of exploring specific information. Her accessible version allowed users to pause automatic updates and refresh data manually when ready.

Motion and animation in data visualizations can be problematic for users with vestibular disorders, who may experience dizziness or nausea from moving content. Elena learned to provide controls that allowed users to disable animations and to use motion sparingly and purposefully in her designs. When she did include animations, she ensured they served a clear functional purpose and could be paused or disabled.

Auto-playing content poses accessibility challenges for multiple user groups. Screen reader users may have difficulty understanding content that changes while they're trying to read it. Users with cognitive disabilities may find auto-playing content distracting or overwhelming. Elena implemented user controls for all auto-playing content, allowing users to start, stop, and control the pace of dynamic presentations.

4.6 Testing and Validation: Ensuring Real-World Accessibility

4.6.1 Automated and Manual Testing Approaches

Creating accessible data visualizations requires ongoing testing and validation to ensure that theoretical accessibility translates into practical usability. Elena learned that automated testing tools, while valuable, only catch about 30% of accessibility issues . The remaining 70% require manual testing and, most importantly, feedback from actual users with disabilities.

Automated testing tools provide a good starting point for accessibility evaluation. Browser extensions like axe DevTools and WAVE can quickly identify common issues like missing alternative text, insufficient color contrast, or improper heading structure. Elena incorporated these tools into her regular workflow, running accessibility checks alongside her usual quality assurance processes.

4.6.2 Comprehensive Automated Testing Strategies

Elena developed a systematic approach to automated testing that went beyond basic accessibility scanners. She used multiple tools to catch different types of issues: axe DevTools for comprehensive WCAG compliance checking, WAVE for visual feedback on accessibility problems, and Lighthouse for performance and accessibility scoring. Each tool provided different insights and caught issues that others missed.

Color contrast testing became a regular part of Elena's design process. She used tools like the WebAIM Contrast Checker and Colour Contrast Analyser to verify that all text and graphical elements met WCAG requirements. She also tested her visualizations with color blindness simulators to ensure that information remained distinguishable for users with different types of color vision deficiency.

Keyboard navigation testing required Elena to unplug her mouse and navigate her entire dashboard using only keyboard controls. This manual testing revealed issues that automated tools couldn't detect: illogical tab order, missing focus indicators, and functionality that wasn't available through keyboard shortcuts. She developed a systematic testing protocol that covered all interactive elements and user workflows.

4.6.3 Manual Testing Methodologies

Manual testing involves using your visualization the way users with disabilities would. This means navigating with only a keyboard, testing with screen reader software, and evaluating the experience at high magnification levels. Elena spent time learning to use NVDA, a free screen reader for Windows, and VoiceOver, the screen reader built into macOS. Initially awkward and slow, this testing revealed issues that automated tools missed and gave her genuine insight into the screen reader user experience.

Screen reader testing taught Elena about the importance of proper markup and logical content structure. She learned that screen readers navigate through content using headings, landmarks, and other semantic elements. Her original dashboard, which relied heavily on visual layout to convey structure, was confusing and difficult to navigate with a screen reader. Her redesigned version used proper HTML semantics to create a logical, navigable structure.

Magnification testing revealed issues with responsive design and layout flexibility. Elena tested her dashboard at various zoom levels, from 200% to 400%, to ensure that content remained readable and functional for users with low vision. She discovered that fixed-width layouts often broke at high magnification levels, leading her to adopt flexible, responsive design approaches.

4.6.4 Color and Contrast Testing in Real-World Conditions

Color and contrast testing goes beyond automated checks to consider real-world viewing conditions. Elena tested her dashboard on various devices, in different lighting conditions, and with color blindness simulation tools. She discovered that colors that looked distinct on her high-quality monitor became indistinguishable on older displays or in bright sunlight.

Environmental testing became part of Elena's accessibility validation process. She tested her visualizations on mobile devices in bright outdoor lighting, on older monitors with poor color reproduction, and on high-contrast displays used by some users with low vision. These tests revealed the importance of designing for the worst-case scenario rather than optimal viewing conditions.

Temporal testing considered how accessibility might change over time. Elena tested her dashboard during different times of day, recognizing that user fatigue and environmental conditions could affect accessibility. She also considered how accessibility might degrade as users' abilities changed due to aging, temporary injuries, or progressive conditions.

4.6.5 User Testing with People with Disabilities

The most valuable accessibility testing involves real users with disabilities. Elena partnered with local disability advocacy organizations to recruit volunteers for user testing sessions. These sessions revealed insights that no automated tool or guideline could provide. For example, she learned that screen reader users appreciated when data tables included summary information at the beginning, allowing them to quickly understand the scope and organization of the data before diving into details.

4.6.6 Recruiting and Working with Disability Communities

User testing with people with disabilities requires careful planning and respect for participants' expertise. Elena ensured that testing sessions were held in accessible locations, that participants were compensated for their time, and that the testing process itself was accessible. She learned to ask open-ended questions about participants' experiences rather than leading them toward specific answers.

Building relationships with disability communities became an ongoing part of Elena's accessibility practice. She attended disability advocacy events, participated in accessibility conferences, and maintained connections with users who provided feedback on her work. These relationships provided ongoing insights into how accessibility needs evolved and how new technologies affected user experiences.

The feedback from these testing sessions led to improvements Elena hadn't anticipated. Users suggested adding keyboard shortcuts for common tasks, requested the ability to customize the interface for their specific needs, and provided insights into how they used data visualizations in their daily work. These suggestions improved the dashboard not just for users with disabilities but for all users.

4.6.7 Iterative Testing and Continuous Improvement

Elena learned that accessibility testing isn't a one-time activity but an ongoing process of iteration and improvement. She established regular testing cycles that included automated scans, manual testing, and periodic user feedback sessions. This continuous approach allowed her to catch accessibility issues early and respond to changing user needs and technological developments.

Documentation of testing results became crucial for tracking progress and sharing knowledge with colleagues. Elena maintained detailed records of accessibility issues discovered, solutions implemented, and user feedback received. This documentation helped her learn from each project and provided valuable information for future accessibility efforts.

Accessibility testing integration with development workflows ensured that accessibility remained a priority throughout the design and development process. Elena worked with her development team to incorporate accessibility checks into their continuous integration pipeline, catching issues before they reached production and making accessibility a shared responsibility rather than an afterthought.

4.7 Building Accessibility into Your Workflow

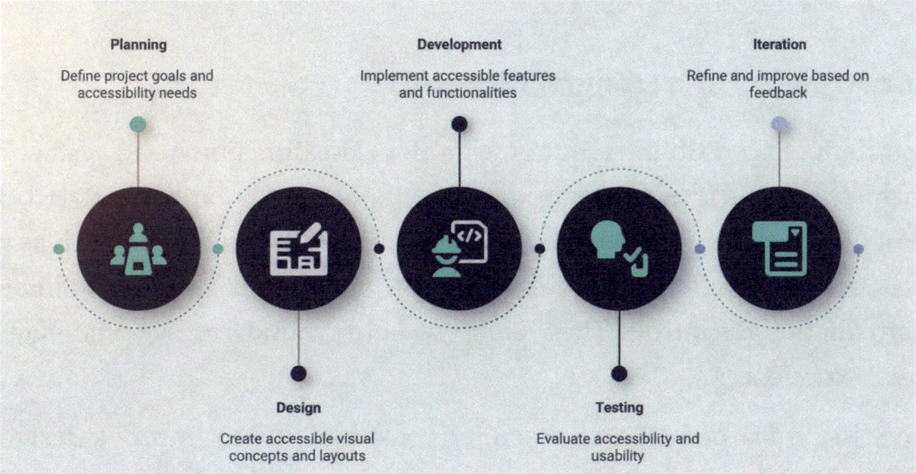

Elena's early attempts at accessible data visualization followed a familiar pattern. She designed charts to look clean and informative, then tried to "add accessibility" at the end—adjusting colors, adding alternative text, or running automated checkers just before publishing. The results were inconsistent. Fixes took longer than expected, some problems couldn't be fully resolved, and the final visualizations often felt patched together rather than thoughtfully designed.

The real change came when Elena recognized that accessibility is not a finishing step but a design approach. Once she began integrating accessibility into her workflow from the start, her process became more efficient, and her visualizations became clearer, more robust, and easier for *everyone* to use.

4.7.1 Planning with Accessibility in Mind

Accessibility now begins in Elena's planning phase. Before opening a design tool, she considers who the visualization is for, how it will be accessed, and under what conditions it will be used. A dashboard viewed on a large monitor in an office presents different challenges than a chart read on a mobile device or accessed through a screen reader. Identifying these contexts early helps Elena anticipate barriers before they become costly to fix.

Rather than treating accessibility needs as edge cases, Elena assumes a diverse audience by default. She plans for users with low vision, color vision deficiencies, motor limitations, and those who rely on assistive technologies. This upfront thinking saves time later and leads to more intentional design decisions throughout the project.

4.7.2 Accessibility as a Design Framework

Elena now defines accessibility requirements alongside functional and aesthetic goals. Inclusive design is no longer optional or implied—it is explicitly stated at the start of each project. Her personas include users with disabilities, such as a screen-reader user navigating charts sequentially, or a keyboard-only user interacting with filters and controls. These personas help ground abstract guidelines in real user experiences.

Over time, Elena learned that accessibility constraints often improve design quality. When color alone cannot communicate meaning, labels, patterns, and structure become stronger. When interactions must work without a mouse, they tend to become simpler and more predictable. Accessibility did not restrict Elena's creativity; it refined it.

4.7.3 Tools, Technology, and Process Integration

Accessibility also influenced Elena's technological choices. She learned that not all visualization tools are equally accessible and that some popular options create barriers that are difficult—or impossible—to overcome. As a result, tool evaluation became part of her accessibility workflow. Support for semantic markup, keyboard navigation, screen readers, and customizable color schemes became essential criteria rather than optional features.

Design artifacts changed as well. Wireframes now include heading structures, reading order, and interaction logic. Prototypes are tested not just visually but with keyboards and screen readers. Design reviews assess accessibility alongside clarity and accuracy, ensuring problems are caught early rather than after release.

4.7.4 Collaboration, Documentation, and Growth

Accessibility work does not happen in isolation. Elena documents her design decisions, testing results, and user feedback so future projects can build on past lessons. She shares guidelines, checklists, and examples with colleagues, helping accessibility knowledge spread beyond a single role or team.

Collaboration became central to her process. Working with developers, content creators, and users with disabilities deepened Elena's understanding of how people actually experience data visualizations. These perspectives shaped better design choices and reinforced the idea that accessibility is a shared responsibility.

4.7.5 Looking Forward

As new tools and technologies emerge—such as AI-assisted alternative text or voice-based data exploration—Elena remains optimistic but cautious. Automation can help, but it cannot replace thoughtful design or meaningful user involvement. Accessibility remains an ongoing practice, not a task to be completed once.

Elena's experience shows that building accessibility into the workflow is not about meeting minimum requirements. It is about designing data communication that is clearer, more flexible, and more trustworthy. When accessibility is part of the process from the start, the result is not just compliant visualization—but better communication for everyone.

4.8 Conclusion

For students beginning their careers in data communication, Elena's experience offers a roadmap for incorporating accessibility into their practice. Start by learning the basics of how people with disabilities use technology. Install a screen reader and spend time navigating websites with your eyes closed. Use keyboard navigation exclusively for a day. These experiences will fundamentally change how you think about digital accessibility.

Learn to use accessibility testing tools and incorporate them into your regular workflow. Automated tools like axe DevTools and WAVE can catch many common issues quickly and easily. Color contrast checkers help ensure your visualizations are readable for users with low vision or color vision deficiencies.

Practice writing alternative text for different types of charts and graphs. This skill requires understanding not just what a visualization shows but what insights it's meant to convey. Good alternative text captures both the literal content and the intended message of a visualization.

Seek out opportunities to learn from people with disabilities. Many communities have disability advocacy organizations that welcome collaboration with students and professionals interested in accessibility. These relationships provide invaluable insights that can't be gained from guidelines or textbooks alone.

Most importantly, approach accessibility as an ongoing practice rather than a one-time requirement. The field of accessibility continues to evolve as technology changes and our understanding of disability and inclusion deepens. Staying current requires continuous learning and engagement with the accessibility community.

Elena's transformation from creating beautiful but inaccessible visualizations to becoming an accessibility advocate illustrates the potential for positive change when we commit to inclusive design. Her COVID-19 dashboard ultimately served its intended purpose—providing crucial health information to help communities make informed decisions—precisely because it was accessible to everyone who needed it.

The choice facing every data communication professional is whether to create visualizations that serve some people well or visualizations that serve all people effectively. Elena's experience demonstrates that this isn't really a choice at all—in our interconnected world, truly effective communication must be accessible communication. The tools, knowledge, and legal frameworks are all in place. What's needed now are professionals committed to putting them into practice.

As you begin your career in data communication, you have the opportunity to be part of a generation that makes accessibility the default rather than an afterthought. Every visualization you create, every dashboard you design, every presentation you give is a chance to include rather than exclude, to clarify rather than confuse, to empower rather than frustrate. The impact of these choices extends far beyond your immediate audience to shape a more inclusive and equitable future for data communication.

The future of data visualization is not just about new technologies or more sophisticated analytical techniques—it's about ensuring that the insights and understanding that data provides are available to everyone who needs them. Elena's story shows us that this future is not only possible but achievable through commitment, learning, and genuine respect for the diversity of human experience and ability.

Chapter 5

Common Ways to Present Data

5.1 Introduction

Jake Martinez was pumped. He'd just discovered that customer satisfaction scores had jumped 15% over the past quarter—huge news that could mean bonuses, promotions, and serious bragging rights. Without thinking twice, he dove into creating the most comprehensive analysis possible: a massive spreadsheet with satisfaction scores broken down by every conceivable category. Forty-seven columns, 312 rows, and enough data to make any analyst's heart sing.

Walking into the marketing team meeting, Jake was ready to blow everyone away with his thorough analysis. Instead, he watched in horror as eyes glazed over while he scrolled through endless screens of numbers. The marketing director looked increasingly frustrated before finally cutting him off: "Jake, I can see you've done amazing work here, but honestly? I have no idea what you're trying to tell me. What's the actual story?"

That painful moment taught Jake the most important lesson of his career: awesome data means absolutely nothing if you can't communicate it effectively. The same breakthrough insights that could change everything become completely useless when buried in the wrong presentation format.

Here's the thing—Jake's data was incredible. But he'd made the classic rookie mistake of thinking that more information automatically equals better communication. Spoiler alert: it doesn't.

This chapter is your guide to avoiding Jake's epic fail. We'll explore the main ways to present data, from simple charts that tell clear stories to comprehensive dashboards that track everything that matters. You'll learn when each format works (and when it spectacularly doesn't), plus how to choose the right approach for any situation. Most importantly, you'll discover how to turn your data insights into communications that get results.

5.2 The Foundation: Clean Data Before Beautiful Presentations

The most elegant visualization in the world becomes worthless—or worse, harmful—when built on unreliable data. Consider what happened when a major retailer's executive team made a million-dollar inventory decision based on a beautifully designed dashboard that showed strong sales trends. The problem? The underlying data included duplicate transactions, missing returns, and incorrectly categorized products. The clean presentation masked dirty data, leading to massive overordering and significant financial losses.

Data quality issues manifest in multiple ways that can undermine even the most carefully crafted presentations. Missing data creates gaps that can skew trends and patterns, making temporary fluctuations appear as meaningful changes. Duplicate records inflate counts and percentages, creating false impressions of growth or performance. Inconsistent formatting across data sources can lead to incorrect categorizations and comparisons. Outdated information mixed with current data creates temporal inconsistencies that confuse rather than clarify trends.

Essential preparation steps include checking for completeness across all required fields, identifying and handling missing values appropriately, removing or flagging duplicate records, and standardizing formats for dates, currencies, and categorical variables. Jake learned to create systematic checklists for data validation that he applied before any analysis or visualization work began.

The investment in data quality pays dividends throughout the presentation process. Clean data makes visualization design easier because patterns are genuine rather than artifacts of data problems. Stakeholder questions focus on insights and implications rather than data accuracy concerns. Most importantly, decisions based on reliable presentations lead to better outcomes, creating a positive cycle where data-driven approaches gain credibility and support throughout the organization.

5.3 Understanding Your Presentation Options

5.3.1 The Container Shapes the Message

Just as the same wine tastes different when served in different glasses, the same data creates different impressions when presented in different formats. A bar chart emphasizes comparisons between categories, while a line chart highlights trends over time. A detailed table provides precision, while an infographic tells a story. Understanding these differences helps you choose the format that best serves your communication goals.

Jake learned this lesson when he took his customer satisfaction data and presented it three different ways to three different audiences. For the executive team, he created a simple line chart showing the overall 15% improvement trend. For the product managers, he built a dashboard comparing satisfaction scores across different product lines. For the customer service team, he provided detailed tables they could use to identify specific areas for improvement.

Each format highlighted different aspects of the same underlying data, and each audience found their version more useful than Jake's original comprehensive spreadsheet. The data hadn't changed, but the presentation format made all the difference in how effectively the information was communicated and used.

5.3.2 Matching Format to Purpose

Effective data presentation starts with understanding what you're trying to accomplish. Are you trying to help someone make a quick decision, monitor ongoing performance, understand a complex relationship, or learn about a new topic? Different purposes require different presentation approaches.

Consider the difference between a monthly sales dashboard used by managers to track performance and an annual report designed to communicate company achievements to shareholders. The dashboard needs to be scannable, actionable, and focused on current metrics. The annual report needs to be comprehensive, persuasive, and accessible to non-experts. The same sales data might appear in both, but the presentation format would be completely different.

Jake developed a simple framework for thinking about presentation purposes: monitoring (ongoing tracking of key metrics), analysis (exploring patterns and relationships), communication (sharing insights with others), and decision-making (providing information to support choices). Each purpose tends to work better with certain presentation formats.

5.4 Graphs and Charts: Visual Summaries That Reveal Patterns

5.4.1 Why Your Brain Loves Charts (And Hates Spreadsheets)

Here's a fun fact: your brain can process visual information about 60,000 times faster than text. That's why Jake's 312-row spreadsheet made people's eyes glaze over, while a simple chart showing the same 15% improvement got everyone excited in about three seconds.

Data is used in all graphs in this chapter presented here.

Table 5.1: Product Line Satisfaction and Purchase Metrics by Region

Product Line	Region	Q1 Satisfaction	Q2 Satisfaction	Repeat Purchase Rate	Issues Reported
Alpha	North	70	81	50	5
Alpha	South	68	78	48	6
Alpha	East	72	83	52	4
Alpha	West	71	82	53	4
Beta	North	65	75	45	7
Beta	South	67	77	47	6
Beta	West	63	72	43	8
Beta	East	66	76	46	7
Gamma	East	70	80	50	5
Gamma	West	68	79	49	6
Gamma	North	69	79	48	5
Delta	South	66	76	46	7
Delta	East	64	74	44	8
Delta	West	67	77	47	6
Epsilon	North	71	82	52	4
Epsilon	South	69	80	50	5
Epsilon	East	70	81	51	4
Epsilon	West	68	79	49	5

Think about it—when you see a line going up, you instantly know something's improving. When you see a tall bar next to short ones, you immediately know which category is winning. Your brain doesn't have to work to understand these patterns; it just gets them automatically.

But here's the catch: this superpower comes with great responsibility. Because people process charts so quickly and trust them so instinctively, a poorly designed chart can mislead just as easily as it can inform. Jake learned to think of charts as powerful tools that needed to be used carefully and honestly.

The goal isn't to make pretty pictures—it's to help people understand your data's story as quickly and accurately as possible. When Jake got this right, his presentations went from confusing data dumps to "aha!" moments that changed how people made decisions.

5.4.2 Bar Charts: The Ultimate "Who's Winning?" Tool

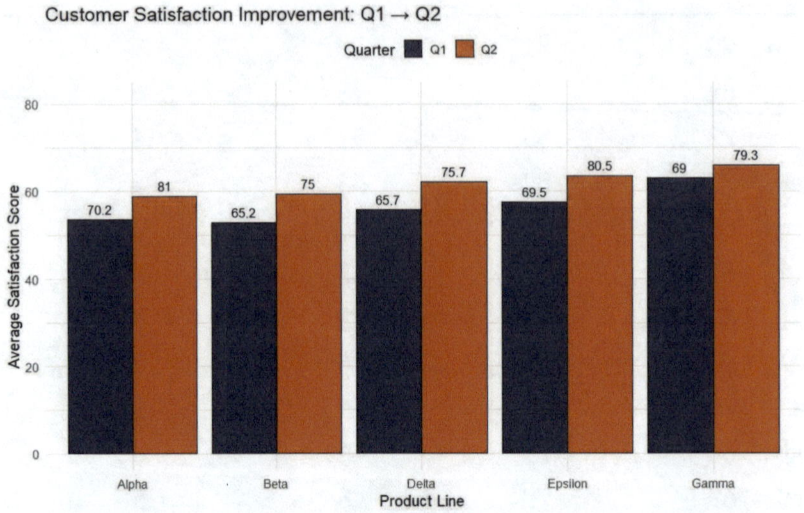

Bar charts are like the scoreboards of data visualization—they instantly show you who's winning, who's losing, and by how much. When Jake needed to show which product, lines had the highest customer satisfaction scores, a bar chart made it impossible to miss. Tall bar = happy customers. Short bar = problem that needs fixing. Simple as that.

The beauty of bar charts is that they're basically foolproof. Your audience doesn't need any special training to understand that taller bars mean bigger numbers. Jake found them perfect for those moments when he needed to make a point quickly and clearly—like showing executives which regions were reaching their targets and which ones needed help.

Here's when bar charts are your best friend: comparing categories (products, regions, teams), showing rankings (top performers vs. bottom performers), and highlighting specific winners or problem areas. They start to break down when you have too many categories (more than about ten bars get overwhelming) or when all your numbers are close together (tiny differences are hard to see).

5.4.3 Line Charts: Your Time Machine for Data

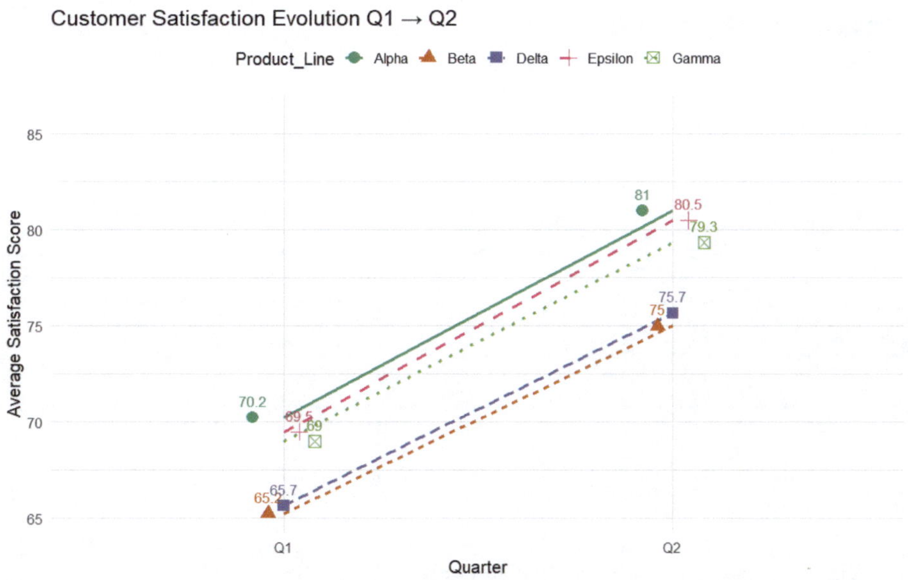

Line charts are perfect for answering the question everyone always asks: "How are we doing compared to last month/quarter/year?" When Jake needed to show how customer satisfaction had evolved over two years, a line chart told the whole story in one glance. Going up = good news. Going down = time to panic. Staying flat = maybe we need to shake things up.

The coolest thing about line charts is that they show you the journey, not just the destination. Jake demonstrates that while satisfaction has improved 15% overall, most of that improvement has happened in the last six months. This wasn't just interesting trivia—it proved that their recent initiatives were working, which helped secure budget for expanding those programs.

Line charts are your go-to when time is part of the story. Stock prices over months, website traffic over weeks, sales performance over quarters—anything where you want to show how things have changed and where they might be heading. They're less useful when you compare different categories at a single point in time (that's bar chart territory).

5.4.4 Scatterplots: The Detective Tool for Hidden Connections

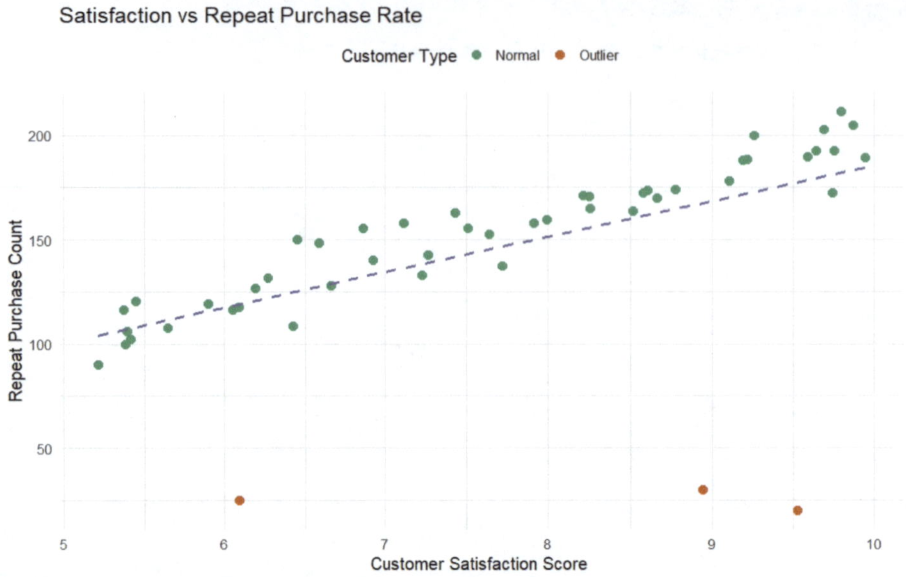

Scatterplots are like detective work for data—they help you figure out if two things are connected or just coincidentally happening at the same time. Jake used them to solve a mystery: did higher customer satisfaction actually lead to more repeat purchases, or was that just wishful thinking?

By plotting satisfaction scores against repeat purchase rates (with each customer as a dot), Jake could see the relationship with his own eyes. The dots formed a clear upward pattern—higher satisfaction really did mean more repeat business. But here's where it got interesting: he also spotted some weird outliers. Customers with high satisfaction but low repeat purchases. What was up with that?

Those outliers turned into Jake's next big project. It turned out that highly satisfied customers in certain regions had trouble reordering because of shipping issues. Fix the shipping, and those satisfied customers become repeat buyers. That's the power of scatterplots—they don't just show you the big picture, they help you spot the exceptions that often lead to the biggest breakthroughs.

5.4.5 Histograms: Understanding Distributions

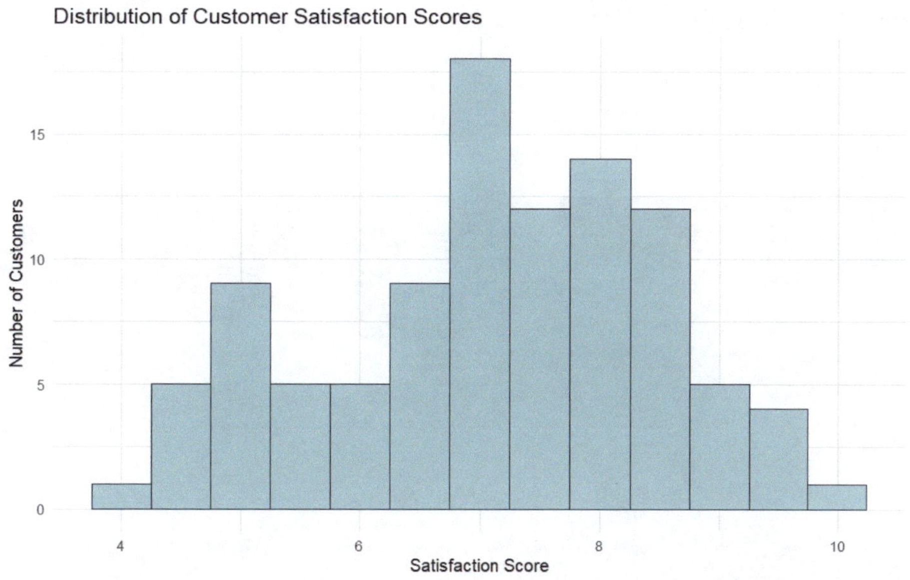

When Jake wanted to understand how customer satisfaction scores were distributed across his customer base, a histogram provided the perfect tool. Unlike bar charts that compare categories, histograms show the frequency distribution of a continuous variable—in this case, how many customers fell into different satisfaction ranges.

The histogram revealed that most customers clustered around moderately high satisfaction scores, with relatively few customers at the extremes of very low or very high satisfaction. This distribution pattern helped Jake understand that while average satisfaction was good, there was room to move more customers from the "satisfied" to "highly satisfied" category.

Histograms work best when you want to understand the shape of your data distribution: Is it normally distributed? Are there outliers? Are there multiple peaks that might indicate different customer segments? Jake found histograms particularly useful for identifying unusual patterns that warranted further investigation.

5.4.6 Boxplots: Comparing Distributions Across Groups

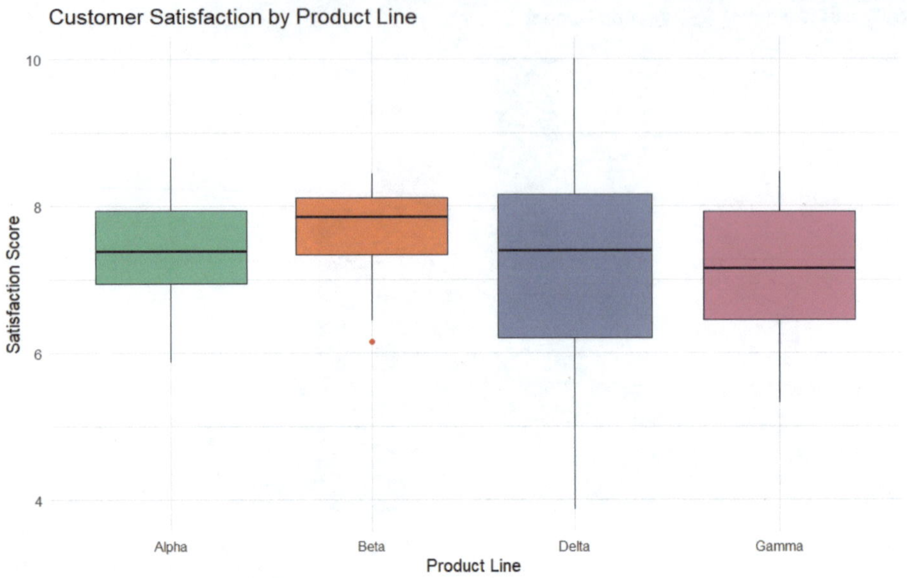

Jake used boxplots when he needed to compare customer satisfaction distributions across different product lines. While bar charts would have shown him the average satisfaction for each product, boxplots revealed much more: the median satisfaction, the range of scores, and whether any products had unusual distributions.

The boxplot for one product line showed that while its average satisfaction was similar to others, it had much more variability—some customers were extremely satisfied while others were quite dissatisfied. This insight prompted Jake to investigate what was causing such inconsistent experiences with that product.

Boxplots excel at revealing differences in distribution shape, spread, and outliers across groups. They're particularly valuable when averages might be misleading because of skewed distributions or when you want to understand the consistency of experiences within each group.

5.4.7 Heatmaps: Visualizing Intensity and Patterns

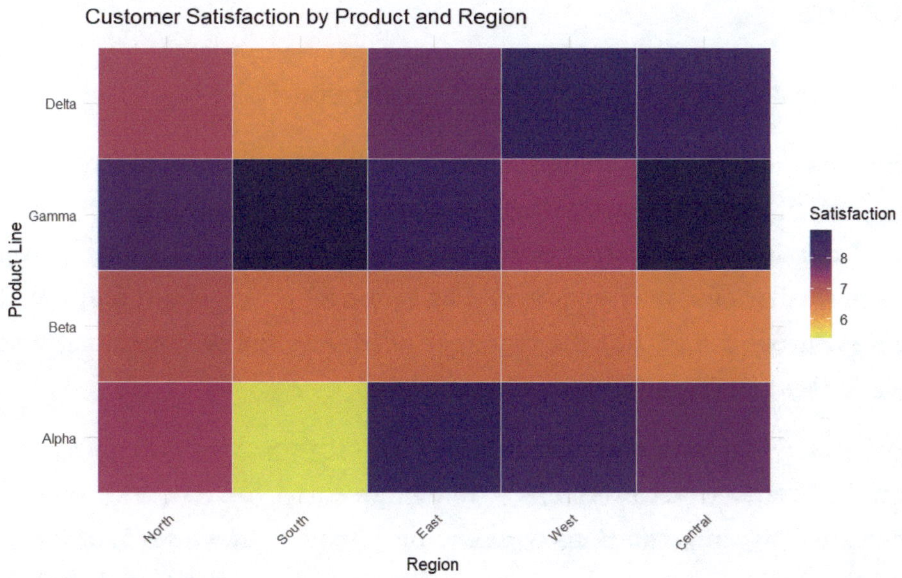

When Jake needed to show customer satisfaction patterns across both product lines and geographic regions simultaneously, a heatmap provided an elegant solution. The heatmap used color intensity to represent satisfaction levels, with darker colors indicating higher satisfaction. This format allowed Jake to quickly identify which product-region combinations were performing best and worst.

Heatmaps work particularly well for showing patterns in two-dimensional data where you want to identify hotspots, clusters, or systematic patterns. Jake could immediately see that certain products performed consistently well across all regions, while others showed significant geographic variation.

The power of heatmaps lies in their ability to make complex patterns visible briefly. However, they work best when you have a clear understanding of what the color coding represents and when the underlying data is appropriate for this type of visualization.

5.5 Tables and Numerical Summaries: When Precision Matters

5.5.1 The Irreplaceable Value of Exact Numbers

While charts excel at revealing patterns and trends, tables serve a different but equally important purpose: providing exact values when precision matters. Jake learned this when a product manager asked for the specific satisfaction score for a particular customer segment. His beautiful charts could show that the score was "around 7.5," but the manager needed to know whether it was 7.52 or 7.48 for budget planning purposes.

Tables work best when your audience needs to look up specific values, perform calculations, or verify exact numbers. They're essential for reference materials, detailed analysis, and situations where approximate values aren't sufficient. Jake found that tables often worked best as supplements to charts rather than replacements for them.

The challenge with tables is that they require more cognitive effort to process than charts. Patterns that are immediately obvious in a bar chart might be completely hidden in a table of numbers. Jake learned to use tables strategically, focusing on situations where precision was more important than pattern recognition.

5.5.2 Raw Data Tables: The Foundation

Raw data tables present information in its most basic form, with rows representing individual observations and columns representing different variables. Jake used raw data tables when analysts needed to perform their own calculations or when transparency about the underlying data was important.

These tables work best for technical audiences who need access to the complete dataset. They're less effective for executive presentations or situations where you want to highlight specific insights. Jake learned to provide raw data tables as appendices or supplementary materials rather than primary presentation tools.

5.5.3 Summary Statistics Tables: Distilling Key Information

Summary statistics tables condense large datasets into key metrics like means, medians, standard deviations, and percentiles. Jake created summary tables to show customer satisfaction statistics for each product line: average score, number of responses, and score ranges.

These tables work well when you need to present multiple metrics for comparison across groups. They're more compact than raw data but more precise than charts. Jake found them particularly useful for technical reports where readers needed specific statistical information.

5.5.4 KPI Tables: Focusing on What Matters Most

Table 5.2: Customer Satisfaction Summary by Product

Product	Responses	Mean	Median	Std Dev	Min	Max
Alpha	20	7.68	7.55	1.31	5.1	9.8
Beta	20	7.46	7.25	1.59	5.2	10.0
Delta	20	7.50	7.70	1.53	5.3	10.0
Gamma	20	7.74	7.85	1.38	5.5	10.0

Key Performance Indicator (KPI) tables present the most important metrics in an easily scanned format. Jake created KPI tables for monthly reports that showed current satisfaction scores, changes from the previous month, and progress toward annual targets.

KPI tables work best when you have a small number of critical metrics that need regular monitoring. They're less effective when you have many metrics or when the relationships between metrics are important. Jake learned to limit KPI tables to no more than 10-12 key metrics to maintain their effectiveness.

5.6 Visual Communications: Infographics and Dashboards

5.6.1 Infographics: Making Data Accessible to Everyone

Jake's first infographic attempt was an absolute train wreck. He tried to squeeze every single customer satisfaction insight into one visual, creating what his colleague kindly called "a beautiful disaster." His second try was pure gold because he finally got it: infographics aren't about showing everything—they're about telling one story really, really well.

Think of infographics as the Instagram posts of the data world. They need to grab attention, communicate quickly, and be shareable. Jake's successful infographic focused on one simple message: "Customer satisfaction is skyrocketing, and here's what that means for you." Clean, clear, and impossible to misunderstand.

Infographics shine when you're talking to people who don't live and breathe data every day. Your customers, the general public, busy executives who have thirty seconds to understand your point—these are your infographic audiences. Jake discovered they were perfect for company newsletters, social media posts, and presentations where he needed to make data feel approachable rather than intimidating.

The secret sauce? Ruthless editing. While dashboards can show multiple metrics and reports can dive deep into details, infographics work best when they laser-focus on one key insight. Jake learned to ask himself: "If someone could only remember one thing from this, what would I want it to be?"

5.6.2 Dashboards: Your Data Command Center

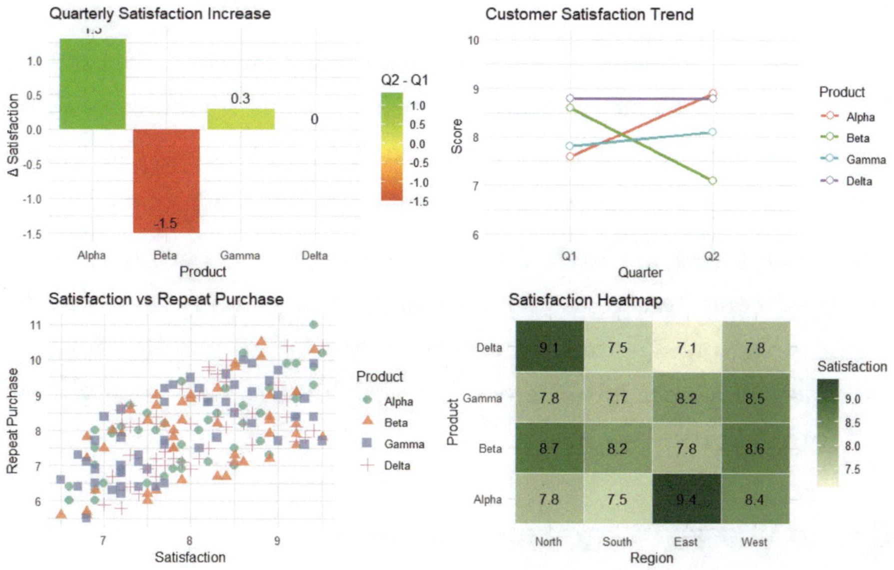

Jake's customer satisfaction dashboard became legendary in his company—not because it was fancy, but because it solved a real problem. Managers were drowning in separate reports and couldn't see the big picture. Jake's dashboard put everything they needed on one screen: current satisfaction scores, trends over time, geographic breakdowns, and response rates.

Think of dashboards as the mission control centers of data communication. They're designed for people who need to monitor multiple things at once and spot problems before they become disasters. Jake's dashboard let managers quickly scan for red flags, then drill down into specifics when something looked off.

The magic of dashboards is that they serve both the "quick check" crowd and the "deep dive" analysts. A manager could glance at it during their morning coffee to see if everything was running smoothly, while an analyst could use the same dashboard to investigate why satisfaction dipped in the Northeast region last month.

5.6.3 Building Dashboards That Actually Get Used

Jake learned the hard way that cramming every possible metric onto a dashboard creates a useless mess. His first version had 47 different charts and looked like a NASA control room. Nobody used it because nobody could figure out what mattered most.

His breakthrough came when he started with just five key metrics—the ones that actually drove decisions. Customer satisfaction score, trend direction, response rate, top problem areas, and geographic performance. Everything else became secondary screens that people could access if they needed more detail.

The best dashboards feel intuitive, like a well-organized smartphone home screen. Jake used consistent colors (red for problems, green for good performance), logical groupings (status at the top, trends in the middle, details at the bottom), and filters that let different users customize their view without breaking the core design.

5.6.4 When to Choose Infographics vs. Dashboards

Jake developed a simple test: if you need to explain it once to a broad audience, go with an infographic. If people need to check it regularly to make decisions, build a dashboard.

Infographics work for annual reports, marketing materials, public communications, and one-time presentations where you want to make data memorable and shareable. Dashboards work for operational monitoring, team meetings, performance reviews, and any situation where the same people need to track the same metrics over time.

The key difference? Infographics are about communication and persuasion. Dashboards are about monitoring and action. Jake found that the best projects often used both—dashboards for the team to track progress, infographics to share successes with the broader organization.

5.7 Written Reports and Text Summaries

5.7.1 The Irreplaceable Role of Explanation

Even the best charts and dashboards often need accompanying text to provide context, interpretation, and recommendations. Jake learned this when executives looked at his customer satisfaction charts and asked, "So what should we do about this?" The data showed what was happening, but it took written analysis to explain why it mattered and what actions should be taken.

Written reports excel at providing context that visual presentations can't convey: background information, methodology explanations, limitations and caveats, and recommendations for action. Jake found that combining strong visuals with clear written explanations created more effective communications than either approach alone.

Reports also serve important documentation functions, creating records of analysis methods, assumptions, and reasoning that can be referenced later. Jake's written reports became valuable resources for future projects and helped new team members understand the context behind ongoing initiatives.

5.7.2 Executive Summaries: Distilling Key Insights

Executive summaries serve as the gateway to longer reports, providing busy readers with the essential information they need to understand key findings and recommendations. Jake learned to write executive summaries that could stand alone while encouraging readers to explore the full report for additional detail.

Effective executive summaries follow a consistent structure: brief background, key findings, implications, and recommended actions. Jake kept his executive summaries to one page and used bullet points and clear headings to make them scannable for time-pressed readers.

5.7.3 Methods and Context Sections

Methods sections explain how analysis was conducted, what data was used, and what limitations should be considered when interpreting results. Jake initially skipped these sections, thinking they were too technical, but learned that they were essential for building credibility and helping readers understand the reliability of his findings.

Context sections provide background information that helps readers understand why the analysis matters and how it fits into broader organizational goals. Jake found that providing this context upfront made his findings more meaningful and actionable for readers.

5.7.4 Key Findings and Recommendations

The heart of any analytical report lies in clearly articulated findings and specific, actionable recommendations. Jake learned to organize findings logically, support them with appropriate evidence, and connect them clearly to business implications.

Recommendations should be specific enough to guide action while being realistic about implementation constraints. Jake's most successful reports included recommendations that specified what should be done, who should do it, and what resources would be required.

5.8 Combining Formats Effectively

5.8.1 The Power of Complementary Presentations

Jake's most effective communications combined multiple presentation formats strategically. His monthly customer satisfaction reports included an executive summary with key charts, detailed tables for analysts who needed specific numbers, and dashboard links for ongoing monitoring.

This multi-format approach served different audience needs within the same communication. Executives could quickly grasp key insights from the summary and charts, analysts could access detailed data from the tables, and managers could use the dashboard for ongoing tracking.

5.8.2 Strategic Layering of Information

Effective combination of formats often follows a layered approach: high-level insights in charts or infographics, supporting detail in tables, and comprehensive context in written sections. Jake learned to guide readers through these layers logically, making it easy to get the level of detail they needed.

The key is ensuring that different formats support rather than contradict each other. Jake learned to check that his charts, tables, and written descriptions all told the same story, even if they emphasized different aspects of that story.

5.9 The Ultimate Cheat Sheet: Choosing the Right Format

5.9.1 Jake's Simple Decision Framework

After months of trial and error (and a few more epic fails), Jake developed a foolproof system for picking the right presentation format. He boiled it down to three questions that never let him down:

1. **What does my audience need to DO with this information?** Make a quick decision? Dive deep into analysis? Monitor ongoing performance? Share with others?
2. **How much time do they have?** Thirty seconds in an elevator? An hour in a meeting? All week to review?
3. **What's their comfort level with data?** Are they data nerds who love spreadsheets, or do they prefer simple visuals?

Once Jake started asking these questions first, his presentation choices became obvious. Executives with two minutes? Simple chart with the key insight. Analysts with time to dig in? Detailed tables and methodology. Team that needs to track progress? They can check daily.

5.9.2 The Quick Reference Guide

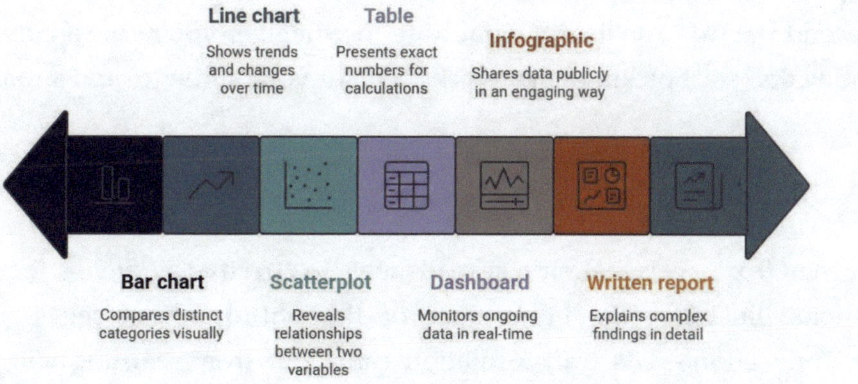

Here's Jake's cheat sheet that he keeps taped to his monitor:

Need to compare things? ◎ Bar chart
Want to show change over time? ◎ Line chart
Looking for hidden relationships? ◎ Scatterplot
Need exact numbers for calculations? ◎ Table
Want ongoing monitoring? ◎ Dashboard
Sharing with the public? ◎ Infographic
Need to explain complex findings? ◎ Written report

Audience has 30 seconds? ◎ Simple chart + one key insight
Audience has 30 minutes? ◎ Multiple charts + brief explanations
Audience has 3 hours? ◎ Comprehensive report with all the details

5.9.3 The Context Reality Check

Jake learned that where and when people use your information matters just as much as what you're presenting. A chart that works perfectly in a quiet conference room might be completely useless on a phone screen during a noisy commute.

Live presentations need big, bold visuals that work from the back of the room. Email reports need to be scannable since people will skim them quickly. Dashboards need to load fast and work on mobile since people check them between meetings.

The best part? Once you start thinking this way, choosing the right format becomes second nature. You'll stop defaulting to whatever you're most comfortable creating and start picking what works best for your audience and situation.

5.10 Conclusion

Jake's journey from overwhelming spreadsheets to effective, audience-focused presentations illustrates the importance of thoughtful format selection in data communication. His transformation came not from learning complex techniques, but from understanding that the same data can and should be presented differently depending on the audience, purpose, and context.

The formats covered in this chapter—charts, tables, infographics, dashboards, and reports—each serve specific purposes and work best in particular situations. Mastering data communication means understanding these strengths and limitations, then choosing the format that best serves your communication goals.

Start by paying attention to how different formats affect your own understanding and decision-making. Notice which presentations help you grasp information quickly and which leave you confused or overwhelmed. Use these observations to guide your own presentation choices.

Practice with different formats using the same dataset. Take a set of data and present it as a chart, a table, an infographic element, and a written summary. Notice how each format emphasizes different aspects of the information and consider which would be most effective for different audiences and purposes.

Remember that effective data presentation is ultimately about serving your audience's needs, not showcasing your technical skills or comprehensive analysis. The best presentation format is the one that helps your audience understand, decide, and act most effectively. Like Jake, you'll find that this audience-focused approach leads to more successful communications and better outcomes for everyone involved.

The goal isn't to master every possible presentation format, but to develop good judgment about when each format serves your communication objectives best. With practice and attention to audience feedback, you'll develop the intuition to choose the right container for your data story every time.

Chapter 6

Ethical and Transparent Communication

6.1 Introduction

Dr. Sarah Chen stood in the conference room at Metropolitan Health Systems, her laptop displaying two different dashboards on the large screen. Both showed the same data about their new AI-powered patient risk assessment system, but they told completely different stories. The first dashboard highlighted their success: emergency readmissions had dropped by 23% over three months. The second revealed a troubling pattern: patients from certain zip codes were being flagged as "high-risk" at rates 40% higher than demographically similar patients from other areas.

The executive committee sat in silence, waiting for her recommendation. The numbers were identical in both presentations, but the implications were worlds apart. One version would allow them to celebrate their innovation and secure additional funding. The other would force them to confront uncomfortable questions about bias and inequality in their supposedly objective system.

"We have a choice," Dr. Chen finally said, her voice steady despite the weight of the moment. "We can tell the success story and risk hiding inequity, or we can tell the harder truth that demands we redesign our approach."

Her dilemma captures the essence of what every data professional faces today: the recognition that how we communicate data is never neutral. Every chart, every color choice, every word in a report carries moral weight. In our data-driven world, the responsibility of those who translate numbers into stories has never been greater.

6.2 Why Ethics Matter in Data Communication

6.2.1 The Hidden Power of Communication Choices

When most people think about data ethics, they imagine privacy breaches or algorithmic bias buried deep in computer code. But some of the most consequential ethical decisions happen not in the algorithms themselves, but in how we choose to communicate their results. A single visualization can hide or reveal discrimination. A carefully worded summary can reassure or mislead. The choice of what to emphasize and what to downplay shapes how audiences understand reality itself.

Consider what happened at a major retailer when their algorithm correctly identified a teenager's pregnancy through her purchasing patterns. The privacy violation didn't occur in the data collection or analysis—it happened when the algorithm's insights were communicated through targeted advertisements that revealed her condition to family members who didn't know. The harm came not from what the system knew, but from how it chose to share that knowledge.

This example illustrates a fundamental principle: data communication is an act of power. When we present data, we're not just sharing information—we're shaping how people understand their world and influencing the decisions they make. With that power comes responsibility.

6.2.2 The High Stakes of Data-Driven Decisions

The stakes are particularly high because data increasingly drives decisions that affect people's lives in profound ways. Healthcare algorithms help determine who receives care. Educational assessments influence which students get opportunities. Financial models decide who qualifies for loans. Criminal justice algorithms inform sentencing decisions. In each case, how the data is communicated can mean the difference between fair treatment and discrimination, between informed decisions and manipulation.

Yet many data professionals receive extensive training in statistical methods and visualization techniques but little guidance on the ethical dimensions of their work. They learn how to make charts that are technically accurate but may not consider whether those charts tell the whole truth. They master the mechanics of data analysis but struggle with questions about what stories they should tell and how to tell them responsibly.

This chapter aims to bridge that gap by exploring the ethical foundations of data communication. We'll examine how seemingly neutral choices about visualization and narrative can have profound moral implications. We'll learn to recognize and address bias in our own work. And we'll develop frameworks for making ethical decisions when the right path isn't immediately clear.

6.3 The Foundation of Ethical Communication

6.3.1 Five Guiding Principles

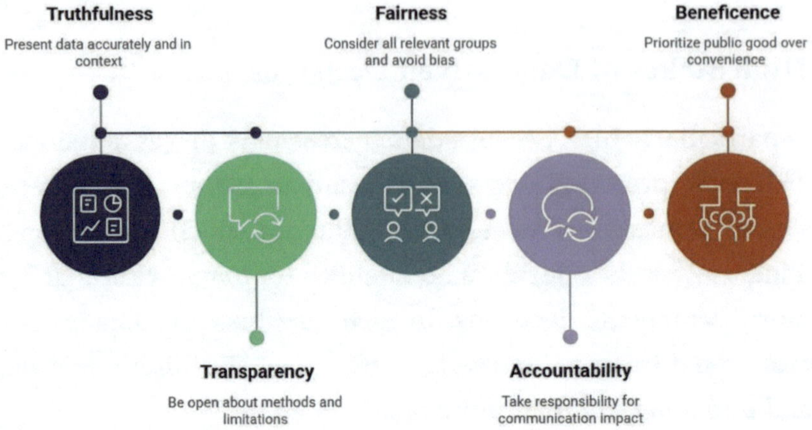

Ethical data communication rests on five fundamental principles that should guide every decision about how to present information. These principles—truthfulness, transparency, fairness, accountability, and beneficence—provide a framework for navigating the complex moral landscape of data storytelling.

Truthfulness means more than just avoiding outright lies. It requires presenting data in ways that promote accurate understanding rather than convenient misinterpretation. A chart with a truncated y-axis might be technically accurate while being fundamentally misleading. A percentage that lacks proper context might be true but deceptive. Truthful communication demands that we consider not just whether our presentations are factually correct, but whether they help audiences understand reality as it actually is.

Transparency involves being open about our methods, limitations, and uncertainties. It means acknowledging what we don't know as clearly as what we do know. When we use data from a survey with a low response rate, transparency requires us to mention that limitation. When our analysis relies on assumptions that might not hold, transparency demands that we explain those assumptions and their potential impact on our conclusions.

Fairness requires us to consider how our communications affect different groups and to avoid perpetuating stereotypes or discrimination. It means presenting data for all relevant populations, not just the ones that make our organization look good. It involves being careful about how we frame comparisons and ensuring that our visualizations don't inadvertently reinforce harmful biases.

Accountability means taking responsibility for the consequences of our communication choices. It requires us to consider how our presentations might be interpreted and misused, and to take steps to prevent harm. When we know that a particular visualization might be misunderstood in ways that could hurt people, accountability demands that we find better ways to communicate the same information.

Beneficence involves actively working to ensure that our communications serve the greater good. It means prioritizing public benefit over organizational convenience and considering the long-term societal implications of our choices. Sometimes this requires us to present uncomfortable truths that challenge existing power structures or reveal inconvenient realities.

6.3.2 Balancing Competing Demands

These principles often come into tension with each other and with practical constraints. Perfect transparency might compromise privacy. Complete fairness might require resources we don't have. Absolute truthfulness might overwhelm audiences with complexity. The art of ethical communication lies in finding ways to honor all these principles while still creating presentations that are useful and accessible.

6.4 Recognizing Bias in Our Stories

6.4.1 The Invisible Influence of Bias

Bias in data communication is like water to a fish—so pervasive that we often don't notice it until someone points it out. It shapes every aspect of how we collect, analyze, and present information, from the questions we choose to ask to the colors we use in our charts. Learning to recognize these biases is the first step toward addressing them.

6.4.2 Visual and Design Bias

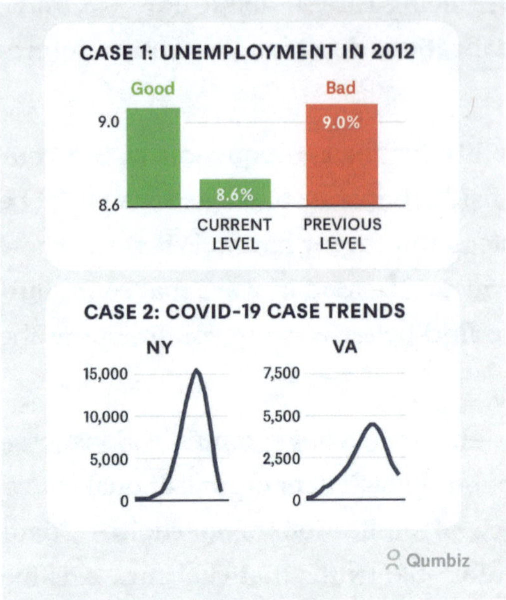

Visual bias is perhaps the most obvious form, though it's still surprisingly common. Consider how Fox News once displayed unemployment data during the 2012 election, using a y-axis that started at 8.6% instead of 0%, making a small decrease from 9.0% to 8.6% appear as a dramatic 50% visual drop. The choice of colors can unconsciously suggest value judgments—using red for one group and green for another in a comparison chart implies that one outcome is "bad" and the other is "good," even when the data represents neutral differences.

Another real example occurred when a major news outlet showed COVID-19 case trends using different scales for different states, making some states' outbreaks appear less severe simply because of the visual presentation. Scale manipulation like this can make small changes appear dramatic or large changes seem insignificant, fundamentally altering how audiences understand the data.

6.4.3 Framing and Narrative Bias

But bias goes much deeper than visual tricks. The way we frame information fundamentally shapes how audiences interpret it. Take the example of a pharmaceutical company that reported their new drug was "50% more effective" than the previous treatment. This sounds impressive until you learn that the previous treatment had a 2% success rate, making the new drug only 3% effective. The framing emphasized relative improvement while hiding the absolute effectiveness.

Similarly, when Theranos reported their blood testing accuracy, they compared their results only to traditional lab methods in ideal conditions, not to the real-world performance that patients actually experienced. This comparative framing bias made their technology appear more revolutionary than it actually was. Showing only population-level statistics while hiding important subgroup variations that reveal inequities represents another common form of aggregation bias—like reporting average test scores that hide the achievement gap between different demographic groups.

Language choices also carry hidden biases. Using phrases like "leads to" or "causes" when describing correlational relationships implies causation where none has been established. Describing the same statistical finding as either "only 15% effective" or "effective for 1 in 7 patients" creates very different impressions, depending on whether we want to emphasize the limitation or the benefit. Even seemingly neutral choices about what information to include or omit can reflect bias—what we choose not to mention often says as much about our perspective as what we highlight.

6.4.4 Personal and Cultural Blind Spots

Perhaps most insidiously, our own backgrounds and experiences create blind spots that we may not even recognize. A data analyst who grew up in an urban environment might unconsciously design visualizations that work well for urban audiences but are confusing or irrelevant for rural populations. A team composed entirely of people from similar backgrounds might miss important perspectives that would be obvious to someone with different experiences.

6.4.5 The Challenge of Unintentional Bias

The challenge is that bias isn't always intentional or malicious. Often, it emerges from practical constraints, unconscious assumptions, or simple oversight. A hospital might focus on aggregate patient satisfaction scores because that's what their reporting system makes easy to generate, not because they're trying to hide disparities. A school district might emphasize test score improvements because that's what their stakeholders expect to see, not because they're deliberately ignoring equity concerns.

Recognizing bias requires developing what researchers call "critical data consciousness"—the ability to step back from our own perspectives and consider how our choices might be perceived by others. It means regularly asking ourselves questions like: Whose voices are represented in this data, and whose are missing? What assumptions am I making about my audience? What would this presentation look like if I approached it from a different angle? How might someone who disagrees with my conclusions interpret this information?

6.5 Strategies for Ethical Communication

6.5.1 Building Systematic Approaches

Developing ethical communication practices requires more than good intentions—it demands systematic approaches and concrete strategies. The most effective organizations build ethics into their processes rather than treating it as an afterthought.

6.5.2 Conducting Regular Bias Audits

One powerful approach is to implement regular bias audits of our visualizations and narratives. Netflix, for example, conducts systematic reviews of how they present viewing data to different stakeholders, ensuring that their success metrics don't inadvertently hide content diversity issues or creator payment disparities.

A practical bias audit checklist includes: checking that axes start at zero unless there's a compelling reason otherwise (and labeling any truncation clearly), ensuring that color choices don't inadvertently suggest value judgments, and verifying that visual elements are proportional to the data they represent. For narratives, it involves reviewing all causal claims—like when a city reported that new bike lanes "caused" reduced traffic accidents, when the data only showed correlation during a period when multiple safety initiatives were implemented simultaneously.

6.5.3 Seeking Diverse Perspectives

Another crucial strategy is to actively seek diverse perspectives on our work. This might involve having team members from different backgrounds review communications before they're released, considering how different stakeholder groups might interpret the same information, or even conducting formal user testing with representative audiences. The goal isn't to achieve consensus—different groups may legitimately have different interpretations of the same data—but to ensure that we understand how our communications might be received and can make informed decisions about how to present information responsibly.

6.5.4 Implementing Balanced Framing

Balanced framing represents another essential technique. Instead of presenting only one perspective on the data, ethical communicators strive to provide multiple viewpoints that help audiences develop a complete understanding. This might mean including both absolute and relative measures when discussing changes over time, presenting both short-term and long-term trends, or comparing performance to multiple benchmarks rather than just one. The goal isn't to be wishy-washy or avoid taking positions, but to provide enough context for audiences to make informed judgments.

6.5.5 Communicating Uncertainty Effectively

Uncertainty communication deserves special attention because it's often overlooked in traditional data presentation training. Ethical communicators clearly acknowledge the limitations of their data and analysis, provide confidence intervals or margins of error when appropriate, and help audiences understand what the analysis can and cannot determine. This doesn't mean overwhelming people with technical details, but rather finding accessible ways to communicate the inherent uncertainty in most data-driven insights.

6.5.6 Protecting Privacy in Communication

Privacy protection in communication requires careful attention to how we aggregate and present information. Even when individual records are protected, the way we communicate insights can sometimes reveal sensitive information about specific people or groups. Effective strategies include using appropriate aggregation levels to prevent identification, applying suppression rules that avoid reporting statistics for very small groups, and being thoughtful about how much demographic detail to include in public reports.

Documentation plays a crucial but often underappreciated role in ethical communication. Maintaining clear records of our communication decisions—including what alternatives we considered and why we made the choices we did—serves multiple purposes. It helps us learn from our experiences and improve our practices over time. It provides accountability when questions arise about our methods or conclusions. And it enables others to understand and build on our work.

6.6 Privacy and Transparency in Practice

6.6.1 The Fundamental Tension

The relationship between privacy and transparency creates one of the most challenging tensions in ethical data communication. On one hand, stakeholders have a right to understand how data-driven systems affect them. On the other hand, protecting individual privacy and sensitive information is a fundamental ethical obligation. Finding the right balance requires careful consideration of what information is truly necessary for understanding and accountability.

6.6.2 Understanding Privacy Breaches in Communication

Privacy breaches in data communication often occur not through direct disclosure of individual records, but through more subtle forms of information leakage. The famous Target pregnancy prediction case illustrates this perfectly: their algorithm identified a teenage customer's pregnancy through purchasing patterns and sent her pregnancy-related coupons, revealing her condition to her family before she had told them herself.

Another real example occurred when the New York City Department of Education published school performance data that was so detailed—including grade level, demographic breakdowns, and specific program participation—that parents could identify individual students with learning disabilities or behavioral issues. Even though no names were used, the combination of characteristics made identification possible in smaller schools. Similarly, when Netflix released "anonymized" viewing data for a research competition, researchers were able to re-identify individual users by cross-referencing the data with public movie ratings on other platforms.

6.6.3 Technical Approaches to Privacy Protection

Effective privacy protection requires thinking carefully about aggregation levels and reporting thresholds. Many organizations adopt k-anonymity principles, ensuring that any combination of demographic characteristics appears for at least k individuals in their reports. Others use differential privacy techniques that add carefully calibrated statistical noise to results, providing mathematical guarantees of privacy protection while preserving overall patterns. Suppression rules that avoid reporting statistics for groups smaller than a certain threshold represent another common approach.

6.6.4 Maintaining Transparency While Protecting Privacy

But privacy protection shouldn't become an excuse for avoiding transparency altogether. There are many ways to provide meaningful insights while protecting sensitive information. Focusing on population-level patterns rather than individual or small-group outcomes often provides the information stakeholders need while maintaining privacy. Emphasizing trends over time rather than point-in-time snapshots can reveal important patterns without enabling identification. Presenting findings in relation to benchmarks or standards rather than absolute values can provide context while protecting sensitive details.

Transparency about methods and limitations is particularly important when privacy constraints limit what information can be shared. If we can't provide certain details because of privacy concerns, we should explain that limitation rather than simply omitting the information without comment. If we've had to aggregate data in ways that might obscure important patterns, we should acknowledge that trade-off. Audiences are generally understanding of privacy constraints when they're explained clearly and honestly.

6.6.5 Algorithmic Transparency Challenges

The challenge becomes more complex when dealing with algorithmic systems that make decisions about people's lives. Stakeholders have legitimate interests in understanding how these systems work, what data they use, and how they might be biased or unfair. But complete algorithmic transparency might compromise competitive advantages, enable gaming of the system, or reveal sensitive information about individuals.

Effective approaches to algorithmic transparency focus on providing the information stakeholders need to assess fairness and accountability without revealing unnecessary details. This might involve explaining the general approach and key components of algorithmic systems without revealing implementation details, reporting comprehensive performance statistics including accuracy across different demographic groups, or providing examples of how algorithms handle edge cases or ambiguous situations.

6.7 The Challenge of AI and Automated Communication

6.7.1 The Rise of AI-Generated Content

Artificial intelligence increasingly generates the dashboards, reports, and visualizations that inform critical decisions across society. While AI can enhance the speed and scale of data communication, it also introduces new ethical challenges that require careful consideration and proactive management.

6.7.2 Bias Amplification in AI Systems

AI systems that automatically generate visualizations may inadvertently perpetuate or amplify existing biases. Google's AI-powered photo service once automatically generated a year-end video for a Black user that was set to upbeat music and featured photos of him being arrested—the algorithm had categorized the arrest photos as "highlights" because they showed multiple people and activity.

Amazon's recruiting AI provides another stark example: the system learned to downgrade resumes that included words like "women's" (as in "women's chess club captain") because the training data reflected historical hiring bias against women in tech. When this AI system generated automated reports about candidate quality, it was essentially amplifying and legitimizing past discrimination. Similarly, when mortgage lending algorithms generate automated risk assessments, they often perpetuate redlining patterns from historical data, presenting discriminatory lending practices as objective risk analysis.

6.7.3 Challenges with Automated Narrative Generation

Natural language generation systems present their own challenges. AI-generated reports may focus on statistically significant findings while omitting important contextual information that human analysts would include. They might use causal language to describe correlational relationships, misleading readers about the strength of evidence. Or they might consistently emphasize certain types of findings over others, creating systematic bias in what information receives attention.

6.7.4 Human-AI Collaboration Complexities

The integration of human judgment with AI capabilities creates additional complexities. Human reviewers may become overly dependent on AI-generated insights, reducing their critical evaluation of results. When humans and AI systems collaborate on communication, it may become unclear who is accountable for errors or biases. There's also a risk that excessive reliance on AI tools may reduce human capabilities for independent analysis and communication over time.

6.7.5 Governance Strategies for AI Communication

Addressing these challenges requires systematic approaches to AI governance in communication. Regular bias testing should assess whether AI-generated visualizations and narratives treat different demographic groups fairly. Accuracy validation should compare AI-generated insights with human expert analysis to identify systematic errors or omissions. Representation analysis should evaluate whether AI systems adequately represent the full diversity of the data and stakeholder perspectives.

6.7.6 The Continuing Need for Human Oversight

Human oversight remains crucial even as AI capabilities advance. Mandatory review processes should require human experts to examine all AI-generated communications before publication, with specific attention to ethical considerations. Clear escalation procedures should define when AI-generated content requires additional human review or expert consultation. Override protocols should enable human experts to modify or reject AI-generated communications when ethical concerns arise.

Transparency about the role of AI in generating insights and presentations is essential for maintaining trust and accountability. Communications should clearly indicate when AI systems have been used and describe their role in the process. The limitations of AI-generated insights and the potential for errors or biases should be explained. The human review processes used to validate and contextualize AI-generated content should be described.

6.8 Building Ethical Organizations

6.8.1 Beyond Individual Ethics

Individual ethical behavior, while necessary, is not sufficient to ensure ethical data communication across an organization. Sustainable ethical practice requires institutional systems, policies, and cultures that consistently prioritize ethical considerations in all communication decisions.

6.8.2 Establishing Clear Standards

Effective organizations start by establishing clear standards for ethical communication that go beyond general principles to provide specific guidance for common situations. These standards might define requirements for visualization truthfulness, such as when axes can be truncated and how such decisions should be labeled. They might establish language guidelines that promote precision in causal claims and uncertainty communication. They might specify minimum standards for providing context, limitations, and alternative interpretations.

6.8.3 Developing Comprehensive Training Programs

Training programs play a crucial role in building organizational capacity for ethical communication. But effective training goes beyond one-time workshops to include ongoing development opportunities that help staff stay current with evolving best practices. Training should be tailored to different roles and responsibilities—data analysts need different skills than executives or communication specialists. It should include practical exercises that help participants apply ethical principles to realistic scenarios they're likely to encounter in their work.

6.8.4 Creating Review and Oversight Processes

Review processes provide another essential component of ethical infrastructure. Many organizations establish communication review boards that include diverse perspectives from different disciplines, backgrounds, and stakeholder groups. These boards have clear authority to require changes to proposed communications or to escalate concerns to senior leadership. They follow defined procedures that include timelines, criteria, and appeal mechanisms.

6.8.5 Fostering Ethical Culture

But perhaps most importantly, ethical organizations create cultures that reward ethical behavior and make it safe for employees to raise concerns about communication practices. This means celebrating instances where staff members identify potential biases or suggest improvements to communication approaches. It means protecting employees who raise ethical concerns from retaliation. And it means ensuring that ethical considerations are given appropriate weight in decision-making processes, even when they conflict with other organizational priorities.

6.8.6 Measuring and Monitoring Progress

Measurement and monitoring systems help organizations track their progress and identify areas for improvement. This might involve developing metrics for assessing transparency, fairness, and accuracy in communications. It could include regular stakeholder surveys to assess trust and satisfaction with organizational communication practices. It should definitely include systematic processes for learning from mistakes and incorporating those lessons into improved policies and procedures.

6.9 Learning from Real-World Cases

6.9.1 Case Study: Healthcare Algorithm Bias

The abstract principles of ethical communication become clearer when we examine how they play out in real-world situations. Consider the case of a major hospital system that implemented an AI algorithm to predict patient risk and allocate care resources. Initial performance reports showed impressive accuracy improvements, but deeper analysis revealed significant disparities in how the algorithm treated patients from different racial backgrounds.

6.9.2 The Communication Dilemma

The hospital faced a classic ethical communication dilemma. They were under pressure to demonstrate the algorithm's success to justify their investment and secure continued funding. But they also had evidence of racial bias that could harm patients and violate their commitment to equitable care. How should they communicate about the algorithm's performance?

The hospital's initial instinct was to focus on the aggregate performance improvements while downplaying the bias findings. After all, the algorithm was performing better overall than previous methods, and the bias issues could presumably be fixed over time. But this approach would have violated several ethical principles. It would have been misleading to present only the positive results without acknowledging the discriminatory effects. It would have been unfair to patients from affected racial groups who deserved to know about the bias. And it would have been unaccountable to hide information that stakeholders needed to make informed decisions about the algorithm's use.

Instead, the hospital chose a more difficult but more ethical path. They developed a comprehensive communication strategy that presented both the algorithm's benefits and its discriminatory effects. They clearly explained the methodology used to detect bias and outlined their plan for addressing it. They committed to regular public reporting on bias mitigation efforts and engaged affected communities in ongoing dialogue about algorithm improvement.

6.9.3 Lessons from the Healthcare Case

This approach required significantly more resources and created some uncomfortable conversations with stakeholders. But it ultimately enhanced rather than undermined trust in the hospital's commitment to ethical care. Patients and community members appreciated the transparency and felt more confident that the hospital was taking bias seriously. Regulators viewed the proactive disclosure favorably. And the hospital's staff felt proud to work for an organization that prioritized ethical principles over convenience.

6.9.4 Case Study: Educational Data Privacy

The case illustrates several important lessons about ethical communication. First, transparency about problems can actually build trust rather than destroy it, especially when it's accompanied by clear plans for improvement. Second, comprehensive ethical communication requires significant resources and organizational commitment—it's not something that can be done as an afterthought. Third, engaging affected communities in dialogue about data-driven systems is essential for developing appropriate responses to bias and discrimination.

Another instructive case involves a school district that implemented a comprehensive student data analytics system to identify students at risk of academic failure. The system showed promising results in enabling early intervention, but it raised concerns about student privacy and the potential for discriminatory labeling.

The district needed to communicate about the program's effectiveness to secure continued funding, but they also had to address community concerns about privacy and bias. Their solution involved developing multiple communication strategies for different audiences. For funders and policymakers, they created aggregate reports that demonstrated program impact while protecting individual student privacy. For parents and community members, they developed plain-language explanations of how the algorithm worked and what data it used. They established regular community forums for discussing the program and addressing concerns, and they implemented clear opt-out procedures with transparent communication about data use.

The district's approach succeeded because it recognized that different stakeholders had different information needs and concerns. Rather than trying to create one-size-fits-all communications, they tailored their approach while maintaining consistent ethical principles across all their communications.

6.10 The Path Forward

6.10.1 An Ongoing Journey

As we've seen throughout this chapter, ethical data communication is not a destination but a journey. The specific challenges we face continue to evolve as technology advances and society becomes increasingly data-driven. New tools create new opportunities for both insight and manipulation. Changing social awareness of bias and discrimination raises the bar for what constitutes ethical practice. Growing public sophistication about data creates both opportunities for more nuanced communication and risks of backlash when organizations fall short of ethical standards.

6.10.2 Your Role as a Future Data Professional

The principles and strategies outlined in this chapter provide a foundation for navigating these challenges, but they require active implementation and continuous refinement. Ethical communication demands ongoing commitment, reflection, and adaptation. It requires us to stay current with evolving best practices and to learn from both our successes and our failures.

Perhaps most importantly, ethical data communication requires us to remember that behind every dataset are real people whose lives may be affected by how we choose to tell their stories. When Dr. Sarah Chen stood before that executive committee, she wasn't just choosing between two visualizations—she was choosing between two visions of her organization's values and responsibilities.

The committee ultimately chose to present both the success story and the bias findings, recognizing that their commitment to ethical care required them to confront uncomfortable truths rather than hide them. That decision reflected the essence of ethical data communication: the courage to tell the whole truth, even when it's difficult.

As you begin your own career in data communication, you'll face similar moments of choice. The frameworks and principles in this chapter can guide your decisions, but ultimately, the responsibility for ethical practice rests with each of us. The power to shape understanding through data communication comes with the obligation to use that power wisely and in service of human flourishing.

The future of our data-driven society depends on professionals who understand that technical accuracy is necessary but not sufficient—that how we communicate about data is as important as the data itself. By embracing ethical principles, implementing systematic practices, and maintaining ongoing commitment to improvement, we can ensure that data serves to illuminate truth and promote justice rather than obscure reality and perpetuate harm.

The choice, as Dr. Chen recognized, is always ours to make. The question is whether we'll have the wisdom and courage to make it well.

6.11 Conclusion

Dr. Sarah Chen's moment of decision at Metropolitan Health Systems represents more than just a choice between two dashboards—it embodies the fundamental challenge facing every data professional in our increasingly connected world. Her committee's ultimate decision to present both the algorithm's success and its discriminatory effects demonstrates that ethical data communication is not about finding perfect solutions, but about having the courage to tell complete truths, even when they're uncomfortable.

Throughout this chapter, we've seen how the seemingly technical act of presenting data is actually deeply moral work. From Fox News's misleading unemployment charts to Target's privacy-violating pregnancy predictions, from Netflix's viewing data audits to Amazon's biased recruiting algorithms, the examples we've explored show that every choice about visualization, framing, and narrative carries ethical weight.

The five principles of ethical communication—truthfulness, transparency, fairness, accountability, and beneficence—provide a framework for navigating these challenges, but they require active implementation and continuous refinement. As we've learned, bias is often invisible to those who create it, privacy can be violated through seemingly innocent aggregations, and AI systems can amplify historical discrimination while appearing objective.

The strategies we've discussed—from conducting regular bias audits to seeking diverse perspectives, from implementing balanced framing to protecting privacy in communication—offer practical tools for ethical practice. But perhaps most importantly, this chapter has emphasized that ethical data communication requires us to remember the human beings behind every dataset, the real lives affected by our choices about how to tell their stories.

As you begin your career in data communication, you'll face your own moments like Dr. Chen's. The frameworks and principles in this chapter can guide your decisions, but ultimately, the responsibility for ethical practice rests with each of us. The future of our data-driven society depends on professionals who understand that technical accuracy is necessary but not sufficient—that how we communicate about data is as important as the data itself.

The power to shape understanding through data communication comes with the obligation to use that power wisely and in service of human flourishing. By embracing ethical principles, implementing systematic practices, and maintaining ongoing commitment to improvement, we can ensure that data serves to illuminate truth and promote justice rather than obscure reality and perpetuate harm.

Chapter 7

Data Storytelling

7.1 Introduction

In today's data-driven world, professionals need more than just numbers—they need to turn data into compelling stories. Data storytelling combines analysis and communication, helping audiences understand insights and act. With so much information available, the challenge is no longer collecting data but interpreting it clearly and communicating it effectively.

This module explores the sophisticated art of audience-centered data storytelling, moving beyond basic visualization to create meaningful connections between data insights and human decision-making. We examine proven frameworks, multi-format integration strategies, and cutting-edge engagement techniques that transform static presentations into dynamic, action-oriented communications.

The evolution of data communication has been remarkable. Traditional approaches focused primarily on accuracy and completeness, often overwhelming audiences with information rather than inspiring action. Modern data storytelling recognizes that effective communication requires emotional resonance alongside analytical precision. Contemporary research reveals that successful data stories share three fundamental characteristics: narrative structure that provides clear beginning, middle, and end guidance; audience alignment that tailors content to specific stakeholder needs and decision-making contexts; and action orientation that creates clear pathways from insight to implementation.

The most compelling data stories achieve what raw statistics cannot: they create emotional connections that motivate audiences to act. When a healthcare administrator sees patient satisfaction scores presented as numbers on a spreadsheet, the information remains abstract. However, when those same scores are woven into a narrative about patient experiences, complete with contextual challenges and clear improvement pathways, the data transforms into a catalyst for organizational change.

7.2 Understanding Your Audience

7.2.1 The Foundation of Effective Communication

Before crafting any data story, successful communicators invest significant effort in understanding their audience's unique characteristics, constraints, and motivations. This audience-first approach fundamentally shapes every aspect of the communication strategy, from the selection of key insights to the choice of presentation format and delivery style.

Understanding your audience goes beyond demographics. You need to know their goals, responsibilities, and how they use information. Executives, for example, focus on strategic outcomes and ROI. They prefer concise summaries and dashboards that support quick decisions, rather than detailed methodology.

Middle management operates in a different context entirely. These stakeholders need operational insights and team performance data that help them navigate day-to-day challenges while contributing to broader organizational goals. Their medium decision authority requires more detailed reports and interactive presentations that allow exploration of underlying factors. They often serve as translators between executive vision and front-line implementation, making their communication needs particularly complex.

Technical teams represent yet another audience category, requiring methodology details, data quality assessments, and implementation specifics. While their formal decision authority may be lower, their expertise makes them critical gatekeepers for successful data-driven initiatives. They prefer technical documentation and code examples that demonstrate analytical rigor and reproducibility.

Understanding your audience also requires consideration of contextual factors that influence receptivity and engagement. Data literacy levels vary dramatically across organizations, requiring careful adjustment of technical complexity and explanation depth. Time constraints shape how much detail audiences can absorb, demanding presentations that respect busy schedules while delivering key insights effectively. Decision timelines create urgency that must be balanced with thoroughness, while current business context influences which insights will resonate most strongly.

7.2.2 Persona Development for Data Storytelling

A persona is a brief written description of a typical audience member that summarizes their role, goals, level of data knowledge, and communication preferences. Creating audience personas helps ensure data stories are tailored to specific stakeholder groups. Effective personas combine basic characteristics (such as job role or decision-making authority) with behavioral insights and preferred communication styles, guiding decisions about what data to present, how much detail to include, and how results should be delivered..

Sarah is a Marketing Director who manages a team of twelve and has moderate comfort with data. In data storytelling, she represents a persona—a model of a typical audience member. She prefers dashboards and visual summaries over detailed statistics. Her main concerns are campaign ROI, customer acquisition costs, and brand performance. She values concise insights with clear action items, especially during budget reviews and strategy meetings.

Developing this persona demonstrates how individual characteristics shape communication needs. Sarah's management responsibilities indicate that she requires information that supports guiding her team, while her limited time makes efficient presentation formats essential. Her moderate technical comfort suggests that complex statistical concepts are best conveyed through analogies and visual representations rather than mathematical formulas.

The persona approach also considers organizational context and decision-making processes. Understanding how Sarah interacts with peers, reports to senior leadership, and manages her team provides essential guidance for designing messages that fit her professional environment. Effective data storytelling, therefore, depends not only on presenting accurate insights but also on tailoring the communication to how the audience will receive and use the information.

7.3 Storytelling Frameworks for Data Communication

7.3.1 The SCQA Method: Structured Narrative Design

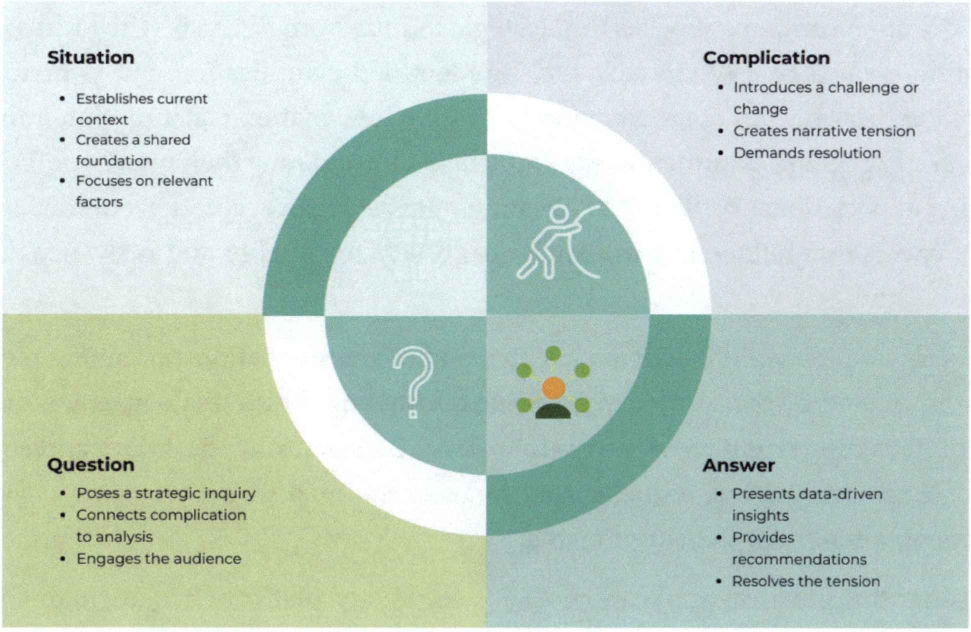

The SCQA framework—Situation, Complication, Question, Answer—provides a logical structure that mirrors natural information processing patterns. Originally developed for consulting presentations, this approach has proven highly effective for data storytelling because it guides audiences through a familiar cognitive journey [[2]].

The Situation component establishes current context and baseline understanding, creating a shared foundation for the narrative that follows. This stage requires careful selection of contextual information that helps audiences understand the environment in which your analysis takes place. Rather than overwhelming listeners with comprehensive background, effective situation-setting focuses on the most relevant factors that influence interpretation of subsequent insights.

The Complication introduces the challenge or change that creates narrative tension, transforming a static description into a dynamic story that demands resolution. This element taps into fundamental human psychology—our natural desire to resolve problems and restore equilibrium. Effective complications are neither trivial nor overwhelming; they represent meaningful challenges that justify the analytical effort while remaining within the audience's sphere of influence or concern.

The Question component poses the strategic inquiry your analysis will address, creating explicit connection between the identified complication and your research approach. This stage transforms passive information consumption into active engagement, as audiences naturally begin formulating their own hypotheses and expectations. Well-crafted questions also establish evaluation criteria for the answers that follow, helping audiences assess the quality and relevance of your insights.

The Answer presents data-driven insights and recommendations, resolving the tension created by the complication while addressing the strategic question directly. This component requires careful balance between analytical rigor and accessible communication, ensuring that complex findings are presented in ways that enable confident decision-making.

Consider this practical application: Our e-commerce platform has maintained steady growth over the past three years, establishing a strong market position through consistent customer acquisition and retention strategies. However, recent market analysis reveals new competitors capturing significant market share through mobile-first approaches that challenge our traditional desktop-focused strategy. How can we adapt our digital approach to maintain competitive advantage in an increasingly mobile marketplace? Our comprehensive user behavior analysis reveals that implementing responsive design and mobile-optimized checkout processes could increase conversion rates substantially, based on current traffic patterns and user interaction data.

7.3.2 The Golden Circle: Purpose-Driven Communication

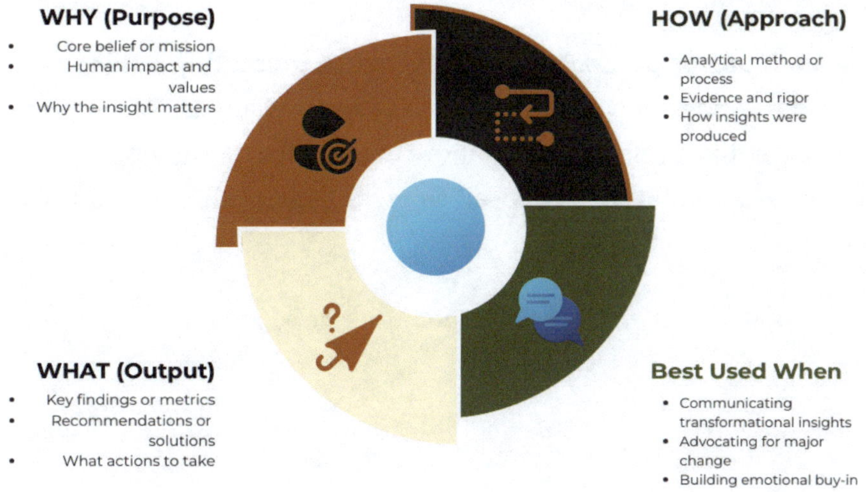

Simon Sinek's Golden Circle framework emphasizes starting with "why" rather than "what," creating emotional connection before presenting technical details [[2]]. This approach recognizes that people make decisions based on beliefs and emotions, then use logic to justify those choices. By beginning with purpose and motivation, data storytellers can create deeper audience engagement that transcends mere information transfer.

The "Why" component articulates the purpose, belief, or motivation driving your analysis, connecting data insights to broader organizational values and individual aspirations. This stage requires moving beyond technical objectives to explore the human impact of your findings. Rather than simply stating that customer satisfaction scores have declined, you might begin by discussing your organization's commitment to exceptional patient care and the personal fulfillment that comes from making a meaningful difference in people's lives.

The "How" element describes your unique approach or methodology, demonstrating the distinctive value of your analytical perspective. This component bridges the gap between inspirational purpose and practical implementation, showing audiences that your insights emerge from rigorous, thoughtful processes that merit confidence and attention.

The "What" presents specific findings, products, or solutions, grounding the inspirational opening in concrete, actionable information. By this stage, audiences are emotionally invested in the outcome and intellectually prepared to engage with detailed recommendations.

This framework proves particularly effective when presenting transformational insights or advocating for significant organizational changes. When proposing major strategic shifts, audiences need more than logical arguments—they need emotional conviction that the proposed changes align with their values and aspirations.

7.3.3 Monroe's Motivated Sequence: Action-Oriented Storytelling

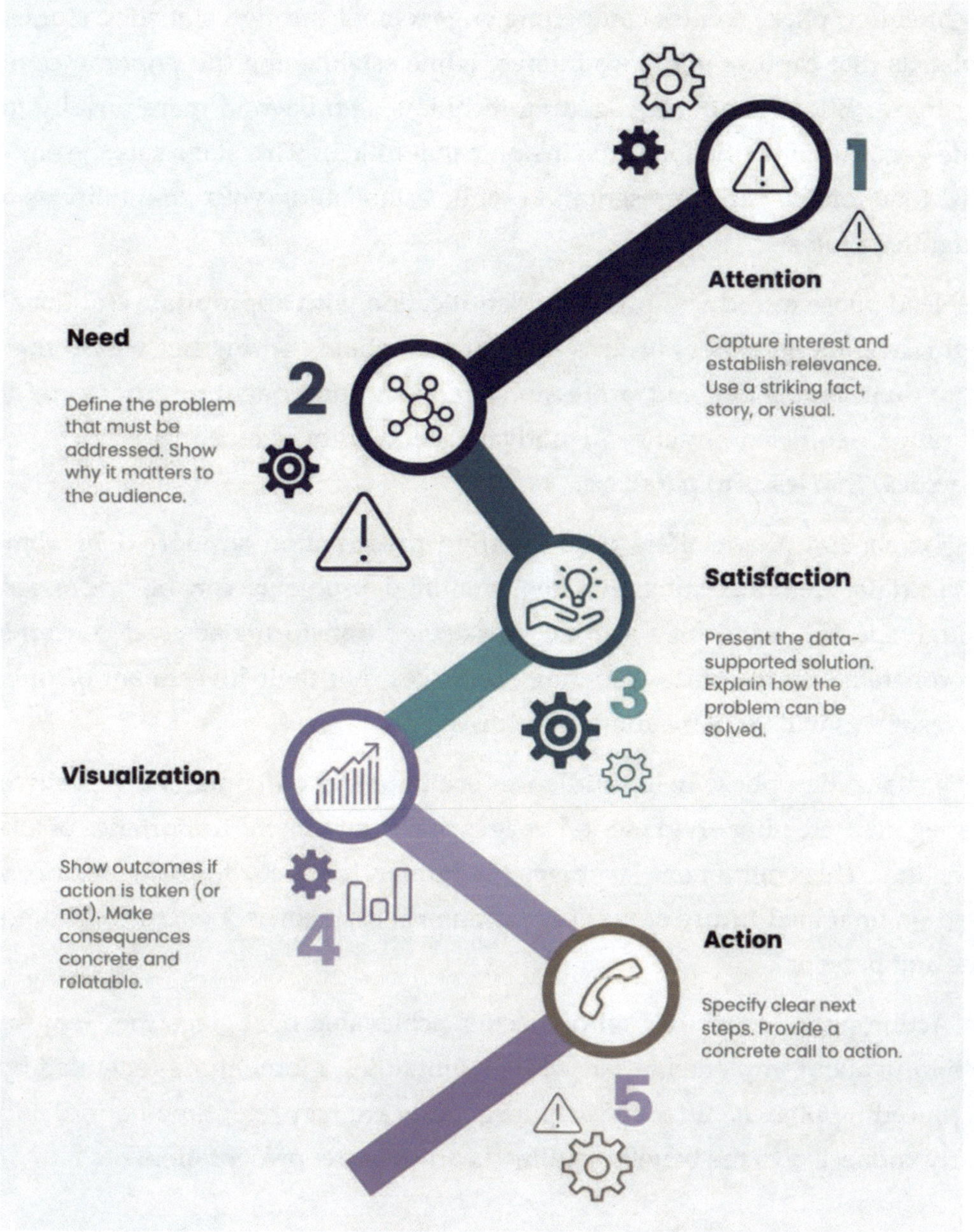

For presentations requiring immediate action, Monroe's Motivated Sequence provides a psychologically-grounded approach to persuasion that systematically builds motivation and removes barriers to implementation [[2]]. This five-phase structure—Attention, Need, Satisfaction, Visualization, Action—leverages established principles of human psychology to maximize persuasive impact.

The Attention phase creates compelling engagement through statistics, stories, or visuals that capture audience interest while establishing the importance of your topic. Effective attention-getting techniques go beyond mere novelty to create genuine curiosity about the insights that follow. This stage sets the emotional tone for the entire presentation while establishing your credibility as a thoughtful analyst.

The Need phase introduces problem identification with appropriate emotional weight, helping audiences understand not just what is wrong but why it matters to them personally and professionally. This component requires careful calibration—sufficient urgency to motivate action without creating overwhelming anxiety that leads to paralysis.

The Satisfaction phase offers clear solution presentation supported by compelling data, demonstrating that the identified problems can be addressed through specific, achievable actions. This stage transforms abstract concerns into concrete opportunities, showing audiences that their investment of time and resources will yield meaningful returns.

The Visualization phase helps audiences see potential outcomes, both positive and negative, creating vivid mental images that reinforce the importance of taking action. This component leverages the human tendency to make decisions based on imagined future scenarios, making abstract consequences feel immediate and personal.

The Action phase concludes with specific, achievable next steps that remove ambiguity about implementation while maintaining momentum generated by the preceding phases. Effective action requests are concrete, time-bound, and clearly connected to the benefits outlined earlier in the presentation.

7.3.4 The Data Story Arc: Narrative Elements for Business Context

The Data Story Arc adapts traditional storytelling elements for business communication, providing a comprehensive framework for complex data presentations that require sustained audience engagement [[3]]. This six-element structure—Context, Business Challenge, Key Data, Discoveries, Recommendation, Call to

Action—creates a complete narrative journey that guides audiences from initial understanding through final commitment.

The Context element introduces the plot, characters, and current state, establishing the business environment in which your analysis takes place. This stage requires strategic selection of background information that helps audiences understand the significance of your findings without overwhelming them with unnecessary detail. Effective context-setting creates a shared foundation for interpretation while highlighting the factors that make your analysis particularly relevant or timely.

The Business Challenge creates narrative tension by identifying problems or opportunities that demand attention and resources. This component transforms static information into dynamic storytelling by introducing elements that require resolution. Well-crafted business challenges are specific enough to guide analytical focus while broad enough to encompass the full scope of your investigation.

The Key Data section develops the story with supporting information, presenting analytical findings in ways that build toward your central insights. This stage requires careful pacing and organization, ensuring that audiences can follow your reasoning process while maintaining engagement with increasingly complex information.

The Discoveries phase illuminates key insights, revealing the breakthrough moments that justify your analytical effort and provide the foundation for subsequent recommendations. This component represents the climax of your data story, where patterns become clear and implications emerge from careful analysis.

The Recommendation section connects insights to business challenges, providing specific guidance that addresses the problems or opportunities identified earlier in your presentation. This stage requires translation of analytical findings into actionable business language that enables confident decision-making.

The Call to Action defines desired audience response, creating clear pathways from understanding to implementation while maintaining the momentum generated by your narrative structure.

7.4 Multi-Format Integration Strategies

Effective data storytelling uses multiple formats instead of just one. Each tool—dashboards, reports, videos, or presentations—serves a different purpose and reaches audiences differently. Using a mix of channels helps people understand and remember the message better.

Interactive dashboards are particularly effective for real-time monitoring and self-service exploration. They allow audiences to investigate data independently while staying connected to the core narrative. Dashboards are ideal for ongoing performance tracking and detailed analysis, but they require careful design to highlight key insights and prevent information overload.

Mobile-friendly reports support field teams and busy executives who need access to essential information regardless of location or device. Small screen constraints encourage clarity and focus on the most important insights, while still providing links or paths to deeper analysis when needed. This ensures that critical information is communicated efficiently, even on the go.

Video narratives leverage a combination of visuals, sound, and storytelling to explain complex concepts or provide training. They are most effective when sequential explanations or personal connections improve comprehension and engagement, making them a powerful tool for audiences who benefit from rich, multisensory learning experiences.

Executive briefings condense complex analyses into high-level summaries suitable for board presentations and strategic decision-making. These formats require careful attention to audience priorities, ensuring that every element contributes directly to the choices leaders must make. Live presentations, in contrast, allow for real-time dialogue, collaboration, and questions, supporting understanding and buy-in. They work best when complemented by other materials that provide additional detail or follow-up resources.

By combining these formats thoughtfully, data communicators can create stories that are accessible, actionable, and memorable. Each tool complements the others, helping audiences not only understand the data but also act on it in ways that support organizational goals.

7.5 Digital Engagement and Interactive Elements

7.5.1 The Interactive Advantage

Digital platforms make audiences active rather than passive viewers. Interactivity isn't just technology—it's a way for people to explore data and understand it more deeply. By filtering, adjusting, or experimenting with information, audiences gain insight and are more likely to act on it.

7.5.2 Implementation Strategies

The success of interactive design depends on aligning tool complexity with audience readiness. Sophisticated features add little value if users lack the skills or motivation to use them. Progressive interaction introduces simple elements first, gradually building toward more advanced capabilities as confidence grows. Purposeful design ensures that every interactive feature serves a communication goal, whether enabling comparison, supporting decision-making, or encouraging exploration. Feedback loops, such as immediate visual or textual responses, sustain engagement by confirming understanding and encouraging continued investigation. In this way, interactivity becomes a guided journey rather than a distracting novelty.

7.5.3 Case Study: Interactive Dashboard Success

A healthcare organization's patient satisfaction dashboard illustrates the impact of thoughtful design. Managers could view their own metrics first, reducing cognitive load and ensuring relevance. Peer comparisons were available without creating unnecessary competition, while direct links to improvement resources connected insights to action. Mobile access allowed busy staff to monitor results on the go. Within six months, dashboard usage rose by 60 percent and patient satisfaction scores improved by 25 percent. This example demonstrates how well-designed interactivity can transform reporting from a periodic obligation into an ongoing driver of improvement.

7.6 Practical Implementation Guide

7.6.1 Getting Started: Your First Data Story

Beginning your data storytelling journey requires systematic approach that builds confidence while developing essential skills. The foundation of effective data storytelling lies in clear communication objectives that guide every subsequent decision about content, format, and delivery approach.

Defining your communication objective requires articulating what you want your audience to think, feel, or do after experiencing your story. This clarity shapes content selection, narrative structure, and success metrics in ways that ensure coherent, purposeful communication. Consider this template: "After this presentation, [specific audience] will [specific action] because they understand [key insight] and believe [compelling reason]."

Framework selection involves choosing the storytelling structure that best matches your objective and audience characteristics. The SCQA method works well for logical, problem-solving presentations that require systematic analysis and clear recommendations. The Golden Circle approach suits inspirational or transformation messages that require emotional engagement before technical explanation. Monroe's Motivated Sequence addresses urgent action requirements that demand immediate response. The Data Story Arc provides comprehensive structure for complex business cases that require sustained engagement and detailed exploration.

Content mapping creates alignment between your chosen framework and available information, ensuring that every element contributes to your communication objective. This process involves identifying the framework elements, determining corresponding content components, and specifying supporting data for each section. For example, a context element might correspond to market overview content supported by industry growth statistics, while a challenge element might involve competitive pressure content supported by market share analysis.

7.6.2 Advanced Implementation Strategies

Multi-stakeholder presentations require modular content design that can be emphasized or de-emphasized based on audience composition and situational factors. Executive modules focus on high-level implications and resource requirements that enable strategic decision-making. Technical modules provide methodology and implementation details that satisfy analytical audiences. Operational modules address process changes and training needs that facilitate successful implementation.

This modular approach enables adaptive presentation that responds to audience dynamics while maintaining narrative coherence and communication effectiveness. Skilled presenters can adjust emphasis and detail level in real-time based on audience engagement and feedback, ensuring that every presentation serves its intended purpose effectively.

Iterative refinement processes develop systematic approaches to improving data stories through experience and feedback. Initial delivery to small, friendly audiences provides opportunities for testing and adjustment without high-stakes consequences. Feedback collection gathers specific improvement suggestions that guide content revision and delivery enhancement. Content revision addresses comprehension and engagement issues identified through feedback analysis. Broader delivery to target audiences proceeds with confidence based on systematic preparation and refinement.

Success metrics establish measurable criteria for evaluating data story effectiveness across multiple dimensions. Engagement metrics assess attention duration, question quality, and participation levels that indicate audience interest and involvement. Comprehension indicators evaluate accurate summary ability and appropriate follow-up questions that demonstrate understanding. Action outcomes measure decision speed, implementation quality, and resource allocation that reflect communication impact.

7.6.3 Common Pitfalls and Solutions

Information overload represents one of the most common challenges in data storytelling, occurring when presenters attempt to share every interesting finding rather than focusing on insights that directly support communication objectives.

The solution involves ruthless prioritization that limits presentations to three to five key insights, ensuring that each element contributes meaningfully to audience understanding and decision-making capability.

Technical complexity creates barriers to understanding when presenters use jargon or advanced statistical concepts without adequate explanation or context. The solution requires developing analogies and simplified explanations for complex concepts, ensuring that technical accuracy does not compromise accessibility or engagement.

Weak calls to action undermine communication effectiveness by ending presentations with vague suggestions rather than specific next steps that enable implementation. The solution involves providing concrete, time-bound actions with clear ownership and accountability, ensuring that insights translate into meaningful organizational change.

7.7 Conclusion

7.7.1 The Future of Data Storytelling

In a world overflowing with data, the ability to shape clear, compelling narratives is becoming essential. The frameworks and techniques outlined here provide a foundation, but true mastery comes through practice, refinement, and adaptation to new technologies and organizational needs. Artificial intelligence and machine learning will increasingly support storytelling by automating routine tasks and enabling personalization, yet the human qualities of empathy, creativity, and strategic judgment will remain at the heart of effective communication.

Looking ahead, data storytelling will emphasize real-time, interactive experiences that foster dialogue between analysts and stakeholders. Immersive tools such as virtual and augmented reality may help audiences grasp complex, multidimensional information, while social and collaborative features will expand opportunities for collective sense-making and shared decision-making.

7.7.2 Key Takeaways

Effective storytelling begins with an audience-first mindset, grounded in a clear understanding of stakeholder needs and motivations. Flexibility in frameworks allows communicators to adapt structure to context, while multi-format integration ensures messages reach diverse audiences across different channels. Interactive tools enhance engagement when they serve the narrative rather than distract from it, and delivery excellence depends on both technical proficiency and adaptive presentation skills.

7.7.3 Integration with Previous Modules

This module builds on the ethical principles established earlier, reinforcing that compelling stories must never compromise accuracy or transparency. Together with prior lessons on technical rigor and visual design, these strategies create a comprehensive approach to data communication. The most powerful stories combine analytical precision with emotional intelligence, bridging complex insights and meaningful action that drives both individual and organizational success.

Chapter 8

Evaluation and Continuous Improvement

8.1 Introduction

Maya Chen had been working as a data analyst for six months when her manager asked her to present quarterly sales results to the executive team. She spent weeks crafting what she thought was the perfect presentation: detailed charts, comprehensive analysis, and polished slides. The presentation went smoothly, executives nodded approvingly, and Maya felt confident she had succeeded.

Three weeks later, Maya discovered that the executives had made a major strategic decision based on completely different data—data that contradicted the trends she had presented. When she asked her manager what had happened, the response was eye-opening: "Your presentation was beautiful, Maya, but nobody really understood what you were trying to tell us. We needed clear recommendations, not just data."

That moment taught Maya a crucial lesson about data communication: creating something that looks good isn't the same as creating something that works. Real success in data communication requires understanding whether your audience actually gets your message, acts on your insights, and achieves better outcomes because of your work.

This chapter explores how to move beyond hoping your communications are effective to knowing they are. We'll examine practical approaches for gathering feedback, measuring impact, and continuously improving your data communication skills. Most importantly, we'll discuss how to build a career-long practice of learning and growth that keeps your skills sharp and relevant in a rapidly changing field.

8.2 Understanding What Success Really Looks Like

8.2.1 Moving Beyond Assumptions

Maya's experience illustrates a common trap in data communication: assuming that a polished presentation equals effective communication. Many professionals focus so intensely on creating visually appealing charts and slides that they forget to verify whether their audience actually understands and can act on the information presented.

Effective evaluation starts with honest questions about what you're really trying to achieve. Are you trying to inform, persuade, or enable action? Are you helping people understand a complex situation, make a decision, or change their behavior? Different goals require different approaches to both communication and evaluation.

Consider the difference between a dashboard designed to monitor ongoing performance and a presentation meant to secure budget approval for a new project. The dashboard succeeds if users can quickly identify problems and take corrective action. The presentation succeeds if decision-makers understand the opportunity, believe in the proposed solution, and approve the requested resources. These different purposes require different evaluation approaches.

8.2.2 Defining Clear Success Criteria

Before you can evaluate effectiveness, you need to define what success looks like for each communication. This means moving beyond vague goals like "inform stakeholders" to specific, measurable outcomes like "enable department heads to identify their top three improvement priorities and develop action plans within one week."

Maya learned to start each project by writing down specific success criteria. For her quarterly sales presentation, success might have meant: "Executives understand which product lines are growing or declining, why these trends are occurring, and what actions they should consider for the next quarter." With clear criteria like these, she could design both her presentation and her evaluation approach to focus on what really mattered.

Success criteria should address three key dimensions: understanding, engagement, and action. Understanding criteria focus on whether your audience grasps the key insights and their implications. Engagement criteria examine whether people pay attention, ask relevant questions, and show genuine interest in the information. Action criteria measure whether communications lead to appropriate decisions, behaviors, or next steps.

8.3 Gathering Meaningful Feedback

8.3.1 The Art of Asking the Right Questions

Getting useful feedback about your data communications requires asking the right questions in the right way. Generic questions like "Was this helpful?" or "Do you have any feedback?" rarely produce actionable insights. Instead, effective evaluation focuses on specific aspects of the communication experience and the outcomes it produces.

Maya developed a simple framework for gathering feedback that focused on three key areas: clarity, usefulness, and confidence. For clarity, she asked questions like "Which parts of the presentation were confusing or unclear?" and "What additional context would have helped you understand the data better?" For usefulness, she explored whether the information helped people make decisions or take action. For confidence, she assessed whether people felt equipped to use the insights in their own work.

The timing of feedback collection significantly impacts its quality and usefulness. Immediate feedback captures fresh impressions and emotional responses, while delayed feedback reveals how well information was retained and whether it influenced subsequent decisions. Maya learned to collect both types, using brief surveys immediately after presentations and follow-up conversations a few weeks later.

8.3.2 Creating Safe Spaces for Honest Input

People often hesitate to provide critical feedback, especially to colleagues or in professional settings. Creating environments where people feel comfortable sharing honest reactions requires deliberate effort and genuine openness to criticism.

Maya found that framing feedback requests as learning opportunities rather than performance evaluations encouraged more honest responses. Instead of asking "How did I do?" she would say "I'm trying to improve my presentations, and your perspective would really help me understand what worked and what didn't." This approach positioned feedback as a collaborative effort to improve communication rather than a judgment of her performance.

Anonymous feedback mechanisms can also encourage honesty, particularly for sensitive topics or hierarchical relationships. Simple online surveys, suggestion boxes, or third-party feedback collection can provide insights that people might not share directly. However, anonymous feedback should supplement, not replace, direct conversation whenever possible.

8.3.3 Learning from Different Perspectives

Different audience members often have vastly different experiences with the same communication. Executives might focus on strategic implications while analysts examine methodological details. Technical experts might appreciate complexity while general audiences prefer simplification. Understanding these varied perspectives helps identify both strengths and improvement opportunities.

Maya began conducting brief interviews with representatives from different audience segments after major presentations. She would speak with one executive, one middle manager, and one front-line employee to understand how the same information landed differently across organizational levels. These conversations revealed that her presentations often worked well for analytical audiences but lost non-technical stakeholders.

Cultural and demographic differences also influence how people receive and interpret data communications. Age, educational background, cultural context, and professional experience all shape how people process information. Effective evaluators seek feedback from diverse perspectives to ensure their communications work for their entire intended audience.

8.4 Simple Ways to Test Effectiveness

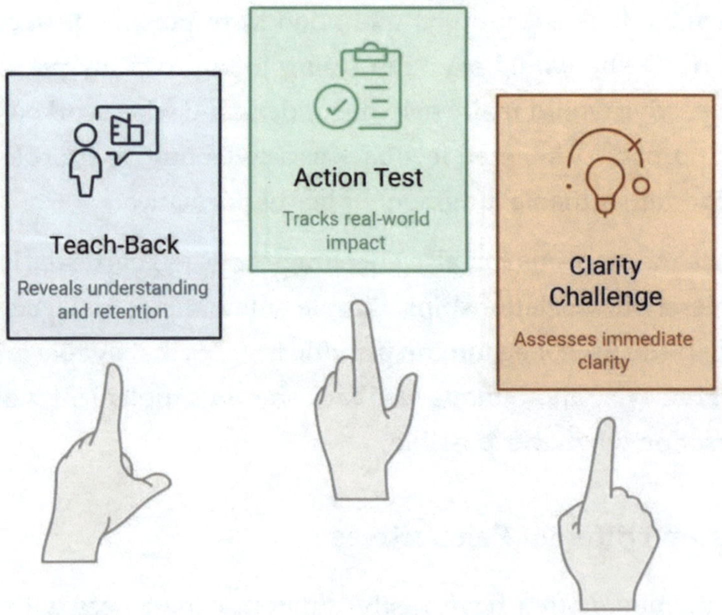

8.4.1 The Five-Minute Follow-Up

One of the most revealing evaluation techniques is also one of the simplest: ask someone to explain back what they understood from your communication. Maya started doing this informally after presentations, asking colleagues to summarize the key points in their own words. The results were often surprising and always illuminating.

This "teach-back" approach reveals not just whether people understood your main points, but how they interpreted and prioritized the information. When Maya asked executives to summarize her quarterly sales presentation, she discovered they had focused entirely on the declining product lines and missed her analysis of emerging opportunities. This insight helped her restructure future presentations to better balance problem identification with solution exploration.

The teach-back technique works for written communications too. Ask colleagues to read your report or dashboard and then explain what they learned without looking back at the original. Pay attention to what they remember, what they forget, and what they misinterpret. These patterns reveal opportunities for clearer organization, better emphasis, and more effective visual design.

8.4.2 The Action Test

The ultimate test of communication effectiveness is whether it enables appropriate action. Maya learned to follow up on her presentations by tracking what decisions were made, what actions were taken, and whether the outcomes aligned with her recommendations.

For routine communications like monthly dashboards, the action test might involve checking whether managers actually use the information to make operational adjustments. For strategic presentations, it might mean tracking whether recommended initiatives receive funding and support. For analytical reports, it might involve seeing whether the insights influence subsequent research or policy decisions.

The action test requires patience, as the impact of communications often unfolds over weeks or months. Maya created a simple tracking system where she noted the key recommendations from each major presentation and then checked back quarterly to see what had actually happened. This long-term perspective helped her understand which communication approaches led to real impact and which generated only temporary interest.

8.4.3 The Clarity Challenge

Maya developed what she called the "clarity challenge" for testing whether her visualizations and reports were truly understandable. She would show her work to someone unfamiliar with the topic—often a colleague from a different department—and ask them to identify the main message within thirty seconds.

This rapid comprehension test reveals whether your key insights are immediately apparent or buried in complexity. If someone can't quickly grasp your main point, your intended audience probably can't either, even if they're more familiar with the subject matter. The clarity challenge forces you to evaluate whether your visual design, information hierarchy, and messaging truly support quick understanding.

The thirty-second timeframe isn't arbitrary—research shows that people form initial impressions of data visualizations within seconds of viewing them. If your main message isn't clear in that initial impression, many audience members will struggle to extract it even with more time and attention.

8.5 Building Better Work Through Iteration

8.5.1 The Power of Version 2.0

Maya's breakthrough in presentation effectiveness came when she started treating every communication as a draft rather than a final product. Instead of spending all her time perfecting a single version, she began creating quick initial versions and then systematically improving them based on feedback and testing.

This iterative approach transformed both the quality of her work and her relationship with the creative process. Instead of feeling pressure to get everything right the first time, she could focus on rapid improvement through multiple cycles of creation, feedback, and refinement. The results were consistently better than her original "perfect" versions.

Iteration works particularly well for recurring communications like monthly reports, quarterly presentations, or ongoing dashboards. Each cycle provides an opportunity to test new approaches, incorporate lessons learned, and gradually optimize for maximum effectiveness. Maya found that her monthly sales reports improved dramatically over six months of systematic iteration, eventually becoming models that other analysts requested to emulate.

8.5.2 Learning from Failure

Maya's most valuable learning experiences came from communications that didn't work as intended. A presentation that confused the audience, a dashboard that nobody used, or a report that led to poor decisions—these failures provided clearer guidance for improvement than her successes.

Effective iteration requires honest analysis of what went wrong and why. Maya developed a simple post-mortem process for communications that missed their mark. She would identify specific problems (unclear charts, missing context, poor organization), explore potential causes (time pressure, unclear objectives, insufficient audience research), and develop targeted improvements for next time.

The key to learning from failure is treating it as information rather than judgment. Failed communications reveal gaps in understanding, skill, or process that can be addressed through focused improvement efforts. Maya found that her biggest professional growth spurts followed her most significant communication failures, as long as she approached them with curiosity rather than defensiveness.

8.5.3 Small Changes, Big Impact

Effective iteration often involves small, targeted changes rather than complete overhauls. Maya learned that adjusting chart types, reorganizing information flow, or clarifying key messages could dramatically improve communication effectiveness without requiring extensive rework.

She developed a systematic approach to identifying high-impact improvements by analyzing feedback patterns. If multiple people mentioned the same confusion point, that became a priority for revision. If certain sections consistently generated questions, she knew they needed clearer explanation or better visual support. If people regularly missed key insights, she examined whether those points were properly emphasized and positioned.

This incremental improvement approach proved more sustainable than attempting major revisions after every presentation. Maya could implement small changes quickly and test their effectiveness immediately, building momentum through visible progress rather than getting overwhelmed by comprehensive redesign projects.

8.6 Developing Your Professional Portfolio

8.6.1 Showcasing Growth Over Perfection

As Maya's skills improved through systematic evaluation and iteration, she began documenting her progress in a professional portfolio. Rather than showcasing only her best work, she learned to tell the story of her development as a data communicator, including examples of how she had improved specific communications over time.

This growth-focused approach proved more compelling to potential employers and collaborators than portfolios that simply displayed polished final products. Hiring managers could see not just what Maya could produce, but how she approached improvement, learned from feedback, and adapted to different challenges. The portfolio demonstrated her capacity for continuous learning—a crucial skill in rapidly evolving fields like data science and analytics.

Maya organized her portfolio around key competencies rather than chronological projects. She included sections on data visualization, presentation design, dashboard development, and written analysis, with each section showing progression from early work to current capabilities. For each major piece, she included brief reflections on what she had learned and how the work had influenced her subsequent approach.

8.6.2 Documenting Your Process

Beyond showcasing final products, Maya's portfolio included documentation of her design and improvement processes. She included before-and-after examples showing how communications evolved through iteration, explanations of design decisions and their rationale, and reflections on lessons learned from both successes and failures.

This process documentation proved valuable for multiple audiences. Potential employers could understand her approach to problem-solving and continuous improvement. Colleagues could learn from her methods and adapt them to their own work. Maya herself found that documenting her process helped her identify patterns in her own development and areas for continued growth.

The portfolio became a living document that Maya updated regularly with new projects, refined examples, and evolving insights. She treated it as both a professional tool and a personal learning resource, using the act of curation and reflection to deepen her understanding of effective data communication principles.

8.6.3 Telling Your Professional Story

Maya learned that an effective portfolio tells a coherent story about professional development and capabilities. Rather than simply collecting examples of good work, she crafted narratives that connected her projects to broader themes of growth, impact, and expertise.

Each portfolio section began with a brief overview of the competency area and Maya's approach to developing skills in that domain. Individual project descriptions included context about the challenge, explanation of the solution approach, and reflection on outcomes and lessons learned. This storytelling approach helped viewers understand not just what Maya had done, but how she thought about data communication challenges and opportunities.

The portfolio also included a professional development section where Maya documented her ongoing learning activities: courses completed, conferences attended, books read, and skills practiced. This section demonstrated her commitment to continuous improvement and helped potential employers understand her trajectory and interests.

8.7 Creating a Personal Learning System

8.7.1 Building Learning Habits

Maya's transformation from struggling presenter to effective communicator didn't happen overnight. It resulted from consistent, deliberate practice supported by systematic learning habits that she developed and maintained over time.

She established a weekly reflection routine where she reviewed recent communications, analyzed feedback received, and identified specific areas for improvement. This regular practice helped her notice patterns in her work, track progress over time, and maintain focus on continuous development rather than just completing immediate tasks.

Maya also created a personal learning library of resources related to data communication, visualization design, and presentation skills. She regularly read blogs, watched tutorials, and studied examples of effective communication from other professionals. This ongoing input provided fresh ideas, exposed her to new techniques, and helped her stay current with evolving best practices.

8.7.2 Seeking Diverse Learning Opportunities

Effective professional development requires exposure to different perspectives, techniques, and challenges. Maya actively sought opportunities to practice data communication in various contexts: presenting to different audiences, working with unfamiliar data types, and collaborating with colleagues from other disciplines.

She volunteered to present at team meetings, offered to help colleagues with their visualization challenges, and participated in cross-functional projects that required communicating complex information to non-technical stakeholders. Each experience provided new learning opportunities and helped her develop versatility in her communication approach.

Maya also engaged with the broader data communication community through online forums, local meetups, and professional conferences. These connections exposed her to cutting-edge techniques, provided feedback on her work, and helped her understand how other professionals approached similar challenges.

8.7.3 Measuring Your Progress

Tracking professional development requires both quantitative and qualitative measures of progress. Maya developed simple metrics for evaluating her improvement: presentation feedback scores, frequency of follow-up questions, time required to create effective visualizations, and success rates for achieving communication objectives.

She also maintained a learning journal where she documented insights, breakthrough moments, and areas of continued challenge. This qualitative record helped her understand not just whether she was improving, but how her thinking about data communication was evolving over time.

Regular self-assessment became part of Maya's professional routine. Every few months, she would review her recent work, compare it to earlier examples, and identify both areas of growth and opportunities for continued development. This systematic reflection helped her maintain momentum and direction in her professional development efforts.

8.8 Putting It All Together

8.8.1 Integration in Daily Practice

The evaluation and improvement practices that transformed Maya's effectiveness didn't require dramatic changes to her daily routine. Instead, she integrated small, consistent practices that gradually built her capabilities and confidence over time.

She began ending each presentation with a brief feedback request, asking one or two specific questions about clarity and usefulness. She started keeping a simple log of communication outcomes, noting what worked well and what could be improved. She established a monthly review process where she examined recent work and planned improvements for upcoming projects.

These practices became natural parts of her workflow rather than additional burdens. The feedback she gathered informed immediate improvements while building her understanding of effective communication principles. The reflection time helped her consolidate learning and maintain focus on continuous development.

8.8.2 Building Organizational Capability

As Maya's skills developed, she began sharing her evaluation and improvement practices with colleagues. She offered to facilitate feedback sessions for other presenters, shared templates for gathering audience input, and mentored junior analysts in developing their communication skills.

This knowledge sharing created positive cycles of improvement throughout her organization. Colleagues began adopting similar practices, leading to generally higher quality communications and more effective use of data in decision-making. Maya found that teaching others reinforced her own learning while contributing to broader organizational capability.

The culture of continuous improvement that emerged from these practices benefited everyone involved. Teams became more comfortable giving and receiving feedback, communications became more effective, and the organization made better use of its analytical capabilities.

8.9 Conclusion

Maya's journey from ineffective to exceptional data communicator illustrates the power of systematic evaluation and continuous improvement. Her transformation didn't require exceptional talent or extensive resources—just commitment to honest assessment, willingness to learn from feedback, and persistence in applying lessons learned.

The practices outlined in this chapter provide a framework for your own development as a data communicator. Start with simple feedback collection and reflection practices. Experiment with different evaluation approaches to find what works best for your context and communication style. Build habits of continuous learning and improvement that will serve you throughout your career.

Remember that becoming an effective data communicator is not a destination but an ongoing journey. The field continues to evolve, audiences develop new expectations, and technology creates new possibilities for communication and engagement. Professionals who embrace evaluation and iteration as core practices will continue to grow and adapt, maintaining their effectiveness and relevance over time.

The investment you make in developing systematic evaluation and improvement practices will pay dividends throughout your career. You'll create more effective communications, build stronger relationships with colleagues and stakeholders, and contribute more meaningfully to organizational success. Most importantly, you'll develop the confidence that comes from knowing your communications truly work—not just hoping they do.

As you begin implementing these practices, remember Maya's key insight: the goal isn't perfection, but continuous improvement. Every communication is an opportunity to learn, every piece of feedback is a gift for growth, and every iteration brings you closer to the kind of data communicator you want to become. The journey starts with your very next presentation, report, or visualization. Make it count.

Made in the USA
Monee, IL
06 November 2026

67912312R00096